# Dating FABRICS 2

## A COLOR GUIDE 1950 – 2000

### Eileen Jahnke Trestain

**American Quilter's Society**

P. O. Box 3290 • Paducah, KY 42002-3290

www.AmericanQuilter.com

# Dedication

*I dedicate this book to my parents, Norman and Patricia Jahnke.*

For my mother, whose bright star has begun to fade from our view, and for my father, whose honor and courage have inspired me all of my life. Their love and marriage has endured through the hardships and laughter over the last 50 years. May all of us be so fortunate.

Located in Paducah, Kentucky, the American Quilter's Society (AQS) is dedicated to promoting the accomplishments of today's quilters. Through its publications and events, AQS strives to honor today's quiltmakers and their work and to inspire future creativity and innovation in quiltmaking.

EDITORS: BARBARA SMITH AND SHELLEY HAWKINS
GRAPHIC DESIGN: ANGELA SCHADE
COVER DESIGN: MICHAEL BUCKINGHAM

**Library of Congress Cataloging-in-Publication Data**
Trestain, Eileen Jahnke.
      Dating fabrics 2: a color guide 1950-2000 / by Eileen Jahnke Trestain.
               p.                   cm.
      Summary: "Information for identification of fabrics from 1950s to 2000. Dating divisions coincide with historical events that influenced styles. Source for studying fashion and clothing trends from the late twentieth century"--Provided by publisher.
      Includes bibliographical references.
      ISBN 1-57432-883-2
      1. Textile fabrics--Dating. 2. Quilts--United States--Dating. 3. Color in the textile industries.
I. Title.
NK9112.T762                2005
746.46'0973'09045--dc22                                 2005010270
                                                                  CIP

Additional copies of this book may be ordered from the American Quilter's Society, PO Box 3290, Paducah, KY 42002-3290; 800-626-5420 (orders only please); or online at www.AQSquilt.com. For all other inquiries, call 270-898-7903.

# Acknowledgments

My grandmother, Jessie Hertel, sewed clothing for clients and first taught me to quilt. Her daughter, my mother, was a professional seamstress throughout the 1960s and 1970s, teaching Bishop sewing and other adult education sewing classes. In the 1990s, she was in another line of work. During vacation, mom and my oldest sister, Colleen, worked in my pattern booths at national shows. Today, Grandma, Mother, and I share our stash with all of you.

Thank you to Roberta Cook whose gift of a 40-year collection of quilt magazines made research so much easier.

Generous friends have volunteered items from their collections. Some lived close enough to share the work. Special thanks to Julie Daly, Sharon Metzler, and Tracy Hill, who sliced their way into my collection for the benefit of this book.

Dear friends have given me love and support when my spirit was weary. Thank you from my heart to every one of you, especially Marjory Peck, Alexandra Henry, Elese Claussen, Nelly Lopes, and my dear sister, Colleen Aemisegger.

And forever and always, there is Dave.

As quilters and fabric collectors, we love the fabric companies who supply us with the materials to produce our art. They have provided us with a lifetime full of color. Thank you to the following companies that have produced the known swatches of fabrics in this book, and to those whom we cannot identify.

Alexander Henry Fabrics, Inc.
American Folk & Fabric Inc.
Andover/Makower Fabrics, Inc.
Bali Fabrics Inc. & Princess Mirah Design
Benartex Inc.
Chanteclaire Fabrics
Classic Cottons/Weilwood, Inc.
Clothworks/Fabric Sales Co.
Cosette Originals
Cranston Print Works Company
Da Gama Textiles
Dan River Inc.
Desert Dye Works
E. E. Schenck/Maywood Studio
Ely & Walker Dry Goods Company
The Erlanger Group, Ltd.
Fabri-Quilt, Inc.
Fabric Country
Fabric Traditions
Hi-Fashion Fabrics Inc.
Hoffman California Fabrics

Island Batik, Inc.
JCPenney
Jeffery Gutcheon
Joy's Fabrics & Quilts
Kona Bay Fabrics
Liberty of London
Manus Fabrics
Marcus Brothers Textiles, Inc.
Michael Miller Fabrics, LLC.
Moda Fabrics
Northcott/Monarch
P&B Textiles
Peter Pan Fabrics, Inc.
RJR Fabrics
Robert Kaufman Company, Inc.
Sears, Roebuck & Company
South Sea Imports
Spiegel
Springs Industries
Timeless Treasures Fabrics, Inc.
VIP by Cranston

# Contents

# Introduction

After the publication of *Dating Fabrics: A Color Guide 1800–1960,* I have had numerous requests for more editions. It seems that people love having a handy reference guide to fabrics. Imagine that!

While I expected the first book to be useful in identifying vintage quilts, it has also found use in unexpected ways. Museums, historical re-enactors, theater production companies, and doll collectors have made it a common reference guide, as in the following examples: Calico buttons made of china or plastic can be compared with the prints pictured in *Dating Fabrics* as a means of establishing their age. Sewing notions and woven rag rugs were often made of textile remnants that are featured in the pages of these books. The age of some books can be determined by comparing the print of their end papers with those of period fabrics, as well as hatboxes and steamer trunks lined in fabrics or papers that are reminiscent of the past. Native American beaded clothing was frequently lined with cotton prints that provide clues in garment dating.

Creating *Dating Fabrics 2* has been a walk down memory lane for me. The time period covers the life of my grandmother when I knew her, the life of my mother, my own life as a young woman, and the early lives of my daughters. The fabric of our daily lives is in this book.

Research included Roberta Cook's collection of quilting magazines. These brought back thoughts of "remember when," like a family quilt does. It was a pleasure to recall the quilters of our time, how they have grown over the years, and what their creative endeavors are now. Perhaps this book will be a "remember when" for you as well. May they all be happy thoughts.

# How to Use This Book

This book was designed as a companion to the previous *Dating Fabrics* book. The layout remains similar, with a color band across the top of the page indicating dates and specific fabric lines, colors, and styles grouped into individual pages.

In general, the fabrics are sorted first by date, then by color. In certain cases, it was more useful to sort by theme of print or type of fabric as opposed to color. Some manufacturers are listed, but not all. This is not intended as a slight or endorsement of any. Many of my personal samples are not identified on the selvage, but have been identified through comparisons with photos in magazines, books, and family histories.

This small encyclopedia only skims the surface of the great quantity of fabric prints produced and used in quilts over the last 50 years. If you have an approximate date for a quilt, turn to the appropriate section to compare the print types and color used in the quilt to confirm or deny your supposition. The fabric dating divisions for this book coincide with turning points in history, which influenced attitudes and style. In making quilts, many quilters of today collect a great deal of fabric to work with, and may draw from a group of fabrics over a long period of time. Quilts may have elements of more than one decade.

Fabric pieces were individually cut and mounted on a page, and the pages were digitally scanned. Printing preparations were made from these scans. The fabric colors shown are as close to the original as today's printing methods allow. There may be minor color discrepancies because the process used to produce color on paper is not exactly the same as that for fabric. Prints are shown actual size because altered scale can be confusing, especially in the case of reproduction fabrics. Few solid-colored fabrics are shown in this book. While the use of these fabrics was a signature of early 1980s quilts, the colors used in any decade matched those of the prints, and quite frankly, there were so many wonderful prints, there was not enough room to include the solids.

For early fabrics, like most of those shown in my previous book, no copyright was registered. By 1900, only some fabric lines made selvage edge identifiers, in addition to paper labels, a regular feature. Items designed before 1929 are now considered public domain. From the 1930s through the early 1960s, printers' marks were hit or miss, making identification of manufacturers difficult. During the 1970s, many fabric manufacturers ceased production, selling out to other companies or closing entirely, while new businesses have risen to take their place. Attempting to follow lines of copyright ownership is a confusing, tangled maze.

Since the 1970s, identifying selvage marks have become a prominent feature. Textile artists were more interested and knowledgeable about the fabrics they purchased, and designers were more likely to demand recognition for their work. Not all fabrics had identifying selvages by the year 2000, and those sold as remainders could be put up on varied labeled bolts. When looking at scraps, whatever the age, most manufacturers' identification was unavailable.

By 2000, quiltmakers looked for specific popular designer names, fabric-line titles, dates, and manufacturers' identification. They checked patterns for proper registration alignment, and bought from the fabric companies who created the type of "hand" they liked in the style of print they desired. Textile artists knew about different qualities of greige goods and were aware of thread counts and types of finish. It is an educated consumer who buys quilting materials today.

Fabric pages from *Dating Fabrics: A Color Guide 1800–1960*

# Poodle Skirts and Atom Bombs

## ABOUT THE PERIOD

With the advent of the atomic age came the beginning of the cold war. The possible use of the moon as a launching site for nuclear weapons, and the one-upmanship of the United States and USSR provided incentive for the two sides to compete in space programs.

Having become president with the passing of Franklin Delano Roosevelt, Harry Truman was president in 1950. By 1953, Dwight Eisenhower was elected president, partly due to the fame of his military service in World War II.

Fought between the years 1950 and 1953, the Korean War ended in a stalemate. Improved airplane designs, tested in the mill of war, and the familiarity with flight shared by returning soldiers, led to advancements in personal travel. International travel encouraged the faster exchange of design ideas between countries. The growth of interstate expressway systems, inspired by the easy transportation of military troops, helped spread ideas across the United States.

The production of the television and its increasing use among the middle to upper class brought favored radio programs into view. The glamour of movies and the styles of European couture houses shown in those movies and on television influenced clothing styles worn by men and women countrywide.

Magazine advertisements and television shows such as *Leave It to Beaver* showed the lady of the house in high heels, pearls, and a "New Look" gown. The reality was that many ladies stayed in the workforce after World War II. Housewives normally spent their days in practical cotton dresses, like Aunt Bea from *The Andy Griffith Show*. However, the need for low-maintenance clothing led to many textile innovations.

## TEXTILE COLORS

After restricted use of dyes during World War II, the desire for more intense colors could finally be satisfied. Dark, saturated colors such as navy, burgundy, orange, red, and yellow were frequently worn in combination prints utilizing a variety of colors.

Nautical prints and the use of red, white, and blue were favored because patriotic feelings in the United States remained strong. Khaki and army green were also popular. Military surplus was available and used to its best advantage. Dresses, curtains, and even wholecloth quilts were sometimes made of recycled parachute silk.

Popular color combinations in fabrics included medium pink, gray, and black with tan or cream. Men's shirts, girls' poodle skirts, women's dresses, and home-interior décor featured these pleasingly peaceful combinations, often utilizing abstract designs.

Alcian blue, which is a light teal, was introduced in 1950. It became a signature color of the 1950s and 1960s and was often used to provide a high contrast with bright pinks or oranges. Blue, green, and turquoise were used together, as were blue and purple, to give an overall feel of coolness to many prints.

Yellow colors tended toward the clear yellow of canary or lemon, but were often mixed in prints with red or black. Red, black, and white was a popular combination. Red tended to be used for floral prints, but also as a background color for prints inspired by different ethnic groups.

Navy blue was sometimes a replacement for black, and solid navy in dresses was considered elegant. Navy blue could be used in combination with red, yellow, pink, green, or white. Brown, green, yellow-gold, gray, and other subdued tones were used for abstract prints and other shapes based in molecular structure. Clothing for home use and daytime social events often utilized bright and colorful prints, but evening wear showed a tendency for solid colors in rich fabrics of satin or velvet.

Gold powder metallic with a binder was printed on the surface of fabrics from the late 1940s through the 1960s. This often dispersed in the first wash, leaving a brown residue on the fabric surface. Some flocking (fuzzy nap) was also a surface application and was easily removed with water, while other flocking was worked into the weave.

Dotted swiss was a sheer fabric used for dresses, but was unsuitable for quiltmaking. The size and scale was a precursor to the pin-dot prints that were popular in the 1970s. Fringe dots consisted of a cut-pile worked into fabrics. Frequently, a tuft of threads was left in a regular pattern, often as part of a plaid. These were occasionally used in quilts.

## FABRIC STYLES

Prior to the 1950s, plain-weave cotton fabrics were usually produced in widths of 36" selvage to selvage. After the 1950s, some manufacturers started producing 45"-wide cotton print, but 36" widths persisted until the late 1970s. The standard width of fabric for silk or wool was 54".

A wide variety of new materials was coming to the market, both in the United States and overseas. These were influenced by the need for low-maintenance fabrics. In addition to cotton, linen, and wool, textiles made of fiberglass, rayon, nylon, acetate, and Lurex metallic yarn were all in use during the 1950s.

Experimentation for the creation of polyester began in the 1930s. Printing designs on polyester was achieved by the use of resin binders, which wore away easily. By 1962, methods were developed for coloring polyesters in the solution phase, referred to as dope dyeing. Polyester was used to make poly-cotton blend, poly-wool, and poly-linen woven fabrics. Extreme fading is evident in many poly-cotton and polyester fabrics. Polyester knit slacks became available in 1960.

In addition to polyester, several other man-made fibers came into common usage. Acrylic was developed in 1950. Acetate was commercially produced in 1955, though it was developed in 1925. Olefin was patented in 1958. Spandex and metallic lamé were introduced in 1960.

Rayon was in experimental stages in the late 1800s and has been commercially produced since 1911. Improvements continued throughout the twentieth century. In the 1930s to 1950s, it was sometimes referred to as poor man's silk and was used in crazy quilts of the era. Production of high-performance, washable rayon in the United States began in 1960. Sometimes it was embellished with beads, sequins, or metallic overprint.

The standard thread count of plain, woven fabrics in 1960 changed from 80 by 80 to 76 by 76 as an effort to reduce production costs. The introduction of the Stork roller-printing machine in 1963 allowed printing of very wide poly-cotton sheeting. These printed sheets were often used as backing for quilts of the 1960s and 1970s.

Special fabric treatments, such as sanforization, were added to cotton fabrics to resist shrinkage and wrinkling. Additives to reduce flammability were increasingly used, especially in children's nightwear.

Rotary transfer screen-printing became the predominant technology for fabric printing in 1954. The printing method change was due partly to the loss of copper rollers from government requisition during World War II, and partly from the expense of engraving and upkeep of the rollers. Rotary screen-printing advancements created smoother blending of color and speed in printing. These changes allowed manufacturers to produce more fabric prints in a shorter time for less money.

The Universal Copyright Convention joined European states in an agreement to respect design innovation in 1953. The United States adopted the resolution in 1955. American fabrics with the universal © copyright symbol were made after 1953. Manufacturers' identification along the fabric edge remained infrequent throughout the decade.

Abstract prints, influenced by the atomic age, were used for furnishings and drapery fabrics in companionship with the Danish modern style. These same style prints were available in plain cottons in the 1940s and 1950s and were utilized for clothing. Both furnishing and plain-weave fabrics featuring these prints can be found in mid-twentieth-century quilts.

Foulards, found in old silk ties, men's pajamas, and underwear, were used for women's dresses and as shirts for the whole family. Light-ground symmetrical geometrics were used for men's underwear and women's dresses and aprons. They are common motifs in quilt fabrics of the era, along with their counterpart colorways.

Home-decorating fabrics such as bark cloth often featured large-scale tropical florals. With a sense of the exotic, these prints were welcomed into the home for draperies and slipcovers by world travelers, returned soldiers, and housewives.

Movies such as *Dumbo* and *The Greatest Show on Earth* inspired circus prints for home décor and children's clothing. The popularity of these motifs continued through the 1960s in bold, contrasting colors. Clown prints were also a fanciful design element for children's wear.

Favorite characters of radio serials went from the movie screen to home television to the dreams and imaginings of many boys and girls. Tom Mix, Gene Autry, Roy Rogers, Dale Evans, the Lone Ranger, and Tonto were the dashing cowboys and friends who became popular design influences for youngsters' bedrooms, pajamas, and everyday shirting.

Stylized folk art such as Dutch, Germanic, and Egyptian motifs became popular print styles. Patterns with a Mexican influence were also favored. These included little donkeys, sombreros, prickly pear cacti, serape-wrapped señors, and smiling señoritas.

Stylized florals, particularly oversized roses, were a feminine accent added to fabrics. While commercially produced, the style was sometimes hand painted. Still, others were embroidered, either in a simple cross-stitch or in a satin stitch of filled and shaded motifs.

Border prints were popular in clothing. Circular border prints were produced to make full skirts without spoiling the pattern by piecing. Border prints along selvages were produced for tablecloths and pillowcases, and could be purchased by the yard. These were sometimes cut for piecing, but were rarely used for borders or sashing in 1950-era quilts.

Scenic prints featuring houses, churches, shops, trees, and sidewalks were popular. These resembled line drawings or etchings, but with added color wash. Scenic prints also included those made for Hawaiian shirts and muumuus, as well as European motifs such as the Eiffel Tower, Big Ben, and the Matterhorn. Reproductions of antique pictorial toiles were a favorite for household textiles.

Plaids were everywhere. They were used for casual shirts, women's aprons, dresses, and full skirts. Winter casual shirts meant cotton or wool flannel plaid. Summer shirts were often lightweight and breathable cotton madras plaid. Gingham, plaid's cousin, was also available. Both were offered in all sizes and a multitude of color shades for clothing, quilts, and tablecloths.

Prints in a cartoon style, featuring objects surrounded by large fields of neutral tone, usually on heavy cotton or linen, were popular for home decorating in the mid-century kitchen. Typical patterns were fruits, vegetables, and kitchen tools. These frequently ended up pieced into block formats or used in quilt backings.

Everyday clothing was often made from printed animal feed sacks and flour sacks. While one feed sack provided an insufficient length of fabric to make an adult's dress, many women saved multiple feed sacks of the same print to complete a garment. Farmers' extension offices around the country provided patterns and directions for varied uses. The seam holes from heavy thread and ink-printed labels are sometimes evident.

Voile and other sheer fabrics were popular in fashion, but rarely seen in quilts due to their fragile nature. Wool fabrics normally used in skirts, jackets, and coats found their way into tied, heavy woolen comforts.

## QUILT STYLES

In some places, the stigma attached to quilts and being poor through the Depression years influenced the decision whether or not to make a quilt. In interviews during documentation days in Texas, many women noted that "poor folks had to make quilts," and that during the war years, blankets were reserved "for the boys overseas," and quilts were for "at home." This stigma remained even into the 1980s, discouraging many otherwise able persons from making quilts.

Prepared quilt kits were an easy way to have a pleasing design for your bedroom décor in the 1950s. Kit quilts were often sold over a long period of time with little variation and could be found countrywide in exactly matching fabrics. Certain indicators distinguish kit quilts from others. These indications include cotton embroidery floss embellishment on appliqués, appliqué designs that feature unified floral designs with matching quilting patterns, and blue placement or quilting indicators that remain after washing. Binding for these quilts was usually commercially prepared bias tape, and these strips were usually pressed open and applied for stems in floral designs. The fold crease on stems is often still evident in many quilts of the style.

Butterflies or pansies were recurring themes for quilts in the era. Both were sold in kit form, but also an abundance of patterns based on these two themes existed in newspaper articles. Sunbonnet Sue and her friends, Overall Jim or Overall Sam, also saw a population explosion. Many children received one of these, with Sue or Jim wearing clothing of scraps to match the child's clothing. Other large-bonneted girls were evident. In the southern states, these were usually referred to as Dutch Girls or Dutch Dolls. Most of these designs were embellished with buttonhole stitch in cotton embroidery.

Double Wedding Ring and Golden Wedding Ring quilts made sentimental gifts and hope chest treasures for brides-to-be. Dresden Plate designs continued, but with variations in the petal shapes and in size. Grandmother's Flower Garden quilts became less frequent than in the 1930s' era. Quilts or quilt tops that had patterns closely related to the swastika, such as Fly Foot and Wind-mill, were covered with new tops or relegated to the closet, attic, or barn.

The proliferation of piecing and appliqué patterns collected from newspapers or purchased from syndicated columns during the 1920s and 1930s were saved and used as references for new quilts from the 1940s to the 1960s. Left-over scraps may have been saved and reused, or recycled from older dresses.

Many of the quilts from the 1940s to the 1960s which are not kit quilts contain a variety of mixed-scale print fabrics in the block piecing, sashing, and borders. Often, these larger-scale blocks have fabrics placed randomly in the block piecing. The movement caused by the mixtures of pattern visually blurs the seam lines. Some quilts from this era are laid out in rainbow color bands, either straight up and down or diagonally across the quilt top. Some quilts have blocks that are a combination of prints with coordinate solids on a light ground. Both of these were classic styles from the 1930s that made the transition into the 1960s.

"Make-do" tied comforters were often a combination of plain weave and furnishing fabrics. They were sometimes randomly pieced, then tied. Other utility quilts were made of wool suiting pieced in rectangles or crazy style. These were often lined with flannel, usually tied, and were very heavy. Backing was often turned to the front of the quilt, rolled over, and hand or machine top-stitched in place along the edge. The rolls were uneven in width. Separate bindings on heavy utility quilts were infrequent.

Cotton batting was the most predominant filler for quilts, though the use of wool was popular in Montana, South Dakota, and North Dakota. The thickness of either material varied, depending on the quilter's budget and desire. For thin quilts, flannel sheeting was a popular quilt filler. Occasionally, a recycled wool blanket was used and made a heavy quilt. Sometimes the sheet or blanket was striped, and these could be seen through outer layers.

Several options were in use for finishing quilts. Many everyday quilts of the mid-twentieth century had the top turned to the front or back, and hand or machine stitched in place. Envelope or knife-edged finishes were also common. Separate bindings were applied to kit quilts and some of the higher quality quilts. In kit quilts, the bias binding came with the kit and may or may not have matched the top exactly. Homemade bindings were bias or straight, depending on the maker's whim. Purchased binding was cut on the bias.

Cowboy novelty

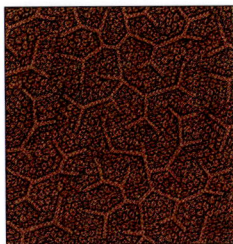

Golden brown with russet

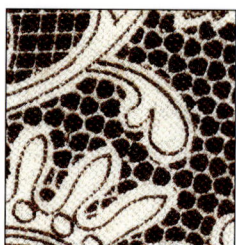

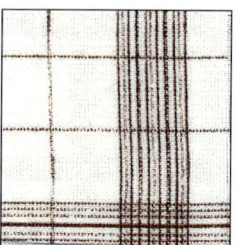

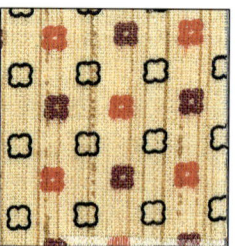

Yellow and brown

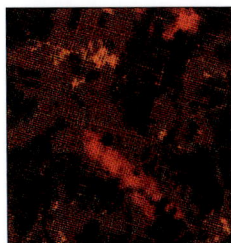

Orange and brown

Orange to melon
gold overprint – oriental influence

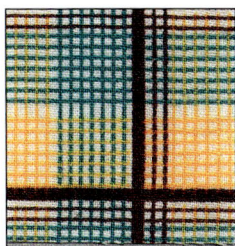

Buttery yellow

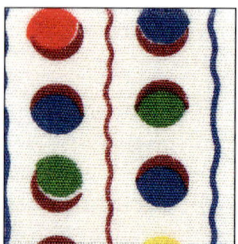

Multicolored with red

Red

Bright pink

Medium-scale pink

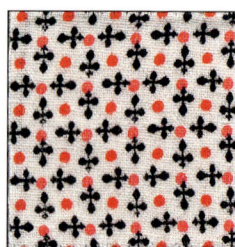

Pink with black, gray, and navy

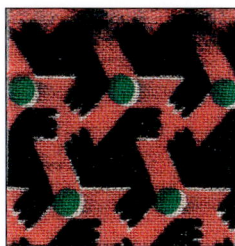

Light pink

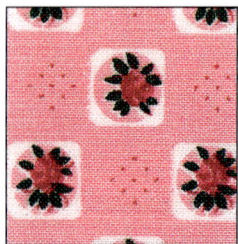

Pink with multicolors

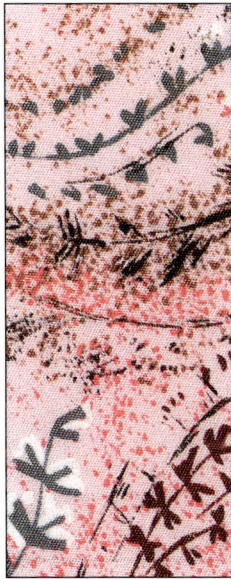

Rose pink

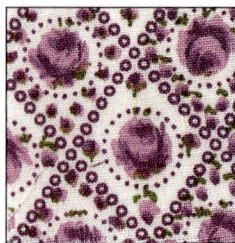

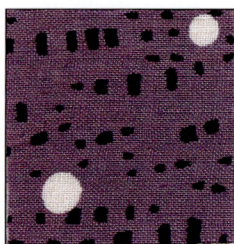

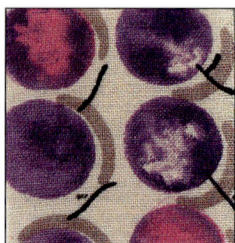

Purple

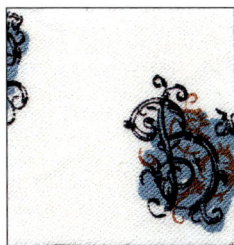

Medium to dark blue

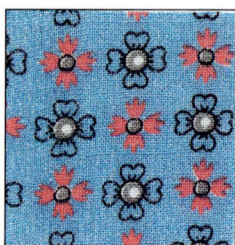

Bright blue and alcian blue

*Dating Fabrics 2: A Color Guide 1950–2000*

Alcian blue

Novelty pictorial kitchen cloth

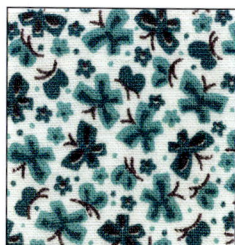

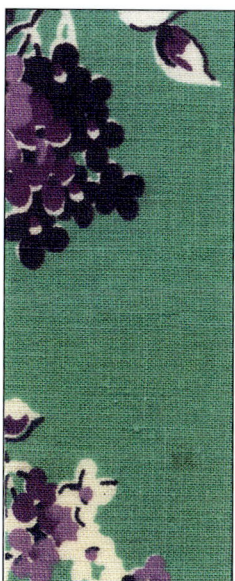

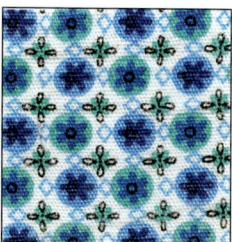

Teal, medium green
Upper right: gold overlay

Light blue to medium teal

Bright green to olive green

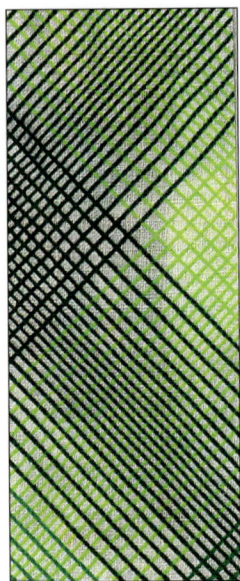

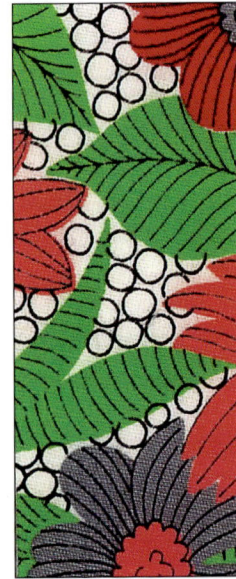

Green and gray or black

*Dating Fabrics 2: A Color Guide 1950–2000*

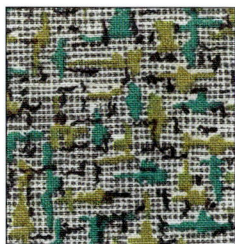

Blue and green combinations

Gray with combinations
Upper left: silver overlay

Black, varied scale with combinations

Black and lights

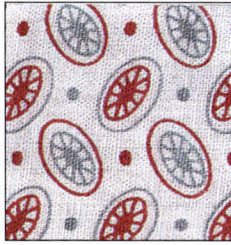

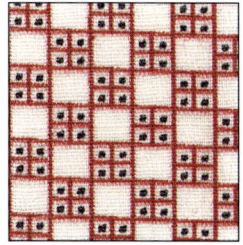

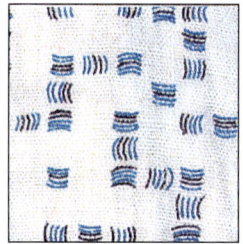

Foulards, men's pajamas, and boxer shorts

Bark cloth

Novelty ethnic – Dutch

Novelty ethnic – Mexican

# *For The Flower Children*

## ABOUT THE PERIOD

President John F. Kennedy was assassinated in 1963. Lyndon Johnson was sworn-in on Air Force One on the way back to Washington DC. In an unpopular move, President Johnson dispatched additional American troops to support the government in South Vietnam. Partly due to antiwar sentiments in the United States, Richard M. Nixon became president in 1969.

The flower child, back-to-nature movement rebelled against the structure of the established hierarchy with peace signs and daisies, which became fabric themes. Outspoken protesters responded with sit-ins and riots. Those who were of an age to be drafted were the strongest antiwar supporters.

Civil rights for people of color were led by Martin Luther King and others. Freedom riders on buses, sit-ins at restaurants, and group marches in Selma, Alabama, and Washington DC kept hopes and efforts for fair and equal treatment in the public eye. It appeared that change was coming in the form of better treatment and equal opportunities for minorities.

The early 1970s' oil embargo by the Organization of the Petroleum Exporting Countries was in protest of the Yom Kippur War. It raised prices of gasoline, materials such as plastics, and petroleum-based fibers like polyester and nylon. Long lines at the gasoline station during rationing made the evening news.

The Freedom Quilting Bee was organized in 1966 as a way for Southern African American women to provide additional income for their families. The Cabin Quilters of West Virginia was established in the 1960s to help Appalachian women sell their craft. Several other organizations formed for the same purpose. Sewing circles and church groups often quilted to raise funds for charities.

Averil Colby, an English needleworker, published quiltmaking books in the 1960s'. Quilting and patchwork taught basic methods from an English point of view, but was marketed in the United States with success. Some of Colby's selective cutting techniques previewed the colorwash quilts of the 1980s. The American Museum opened in Bath, England, in 1961. It was a showcase of American art, especially folk art, and included a collection of quilts.

## TEXTILE COLORS

At the beginning of the 1960s, fabric colors and styles were similar to 1950s' fabrics. Dainty, feminine fabrics of pastel remained in use, but bright, intense colors became increasingly popular toward the end of the 1960s. Light grounds were "in." Turquoise, pink, gray, and yellow remained in high appeal in the early part of the decade. Ladies' casual daywear leaned heavily on floral motifs for prints and colors in a variety of scales. Magazine advertisements displayed work clothing and high fashion using predominately solid colors.

The late 1960s and early 1970s were described as having shocking color combinations, eye-jarring patterns, and large-scale motifs. Orange, purple, red, and black might be used in a single fabric. Acid green, hot pink, tangerine, purple, and turquoise could all be used in a paisley or mod flower print. Whether free form or controlled, as in the use of paisley patterns, these bright, clear colors were unmistakable. Eye-catching DayGlo® fabrics appeared fluorescent, especially under black light.

In contrast, the back-to-nature movement of the late 1960s resulted in colors that imitated natural as opposed to synthetic dyes. Brown, indigo, and madder tones were used in ethnic-style prints. Brown, olive, and gray or black prints were favored for nature prints depicting leaves. Washes of color with abstract outlines were also made in the brown and gold color tones.

Still a favored combination, red, white, and navy blue remained in favor throughout the rest of the century. Patriotism was encouraged with each new military conflict. Deep rose red was occasionally used, and was sometimes a color that bled in washing.

Thin outlines around flowers and stems gave form to color-filled figures. Curlicues of no particular pattern filled in space and defined color areas of some print motifs. Sgraffito prints, based on patterns that have the look of scratches of color, used the style as pattern fill.

In the late 1960s, bandanna prints could be made in any of the available dye hues, in combination with black and white. They were not limited to the formal pattern on a single square of cloth, as used for handkerchiefs, but were printed in haphazard overlapping designs, similar to imitation patchwork. These were used for ladies' and children's blouses and dresses.

While camouflage fabrics found their way into mainstream fashion at the end of the decade, they rarely were used for the quilts of the 1960s. Polyesters, which were dope dyed, took on bright, clear hues. These were usually solid colors, but occasional houndstooth or other especially unique patterns were made in polyester double knit.

## FABRIC STYLES

Knits, leather, vinyl, and paper dresses were all part of the 1960s' fashion world. Polyester double knit began production in 1968 using textured yarns. This fabric was usually 60" wide and sold on a roll, not on a folded bolt. One of its advantages for clothing – resistance to folds and creasing – made it difficult for use in quilts.

The emphasis on arts and youth in the popular culture influenced the pattern designs for many fabric lines in the 1960s. Cubism, surrealism, pointillism, and modernism were all used as design sources in textiles. Overlay of color and transparency in cubist art influenced the same styles in fabric.

Angular prints, reminiscent of modern art, often appeared in bright colors. Op art, houndstooth, and harlequin prints in white and black were also well liked for their dramatic effects. These were more frequently used in suiting than in plain-weave cotton.

Hand-block printing and silk-screen techniques further provided unique motifs and coloration. Loose-weave wraparound skirts and spreads created of fabrics that were hand-block printed in India were popular for wear, and occasionally found their way into quilts. Copies of the Indienne print style on sturdy cotton were made into clothing and quilts for everyday wear.

Tie-dyed patterns on fabric began as individual handmade patterns, but were later produced for the commercial market in repeat pattern. Tie-dyeing was used to color white T-shirts in home studios. Machines for spinning paper and mounted fabrics while dyes were being dropped onto the surface also made for unique pattern designs on fabric.

The flower-child era influenced the daisy and other floral motifs that were popular in fabrics, with styles ranging from cartoon-like designs to watercolor patterns. Mod flowers, like splats of overlapping corona drops of paint, were the signature look of the hippie generation. Flowers of paint, print, and decoupage were on clothing, handbags, and Volkswagens.

Woven textiles of plaids and stripes were used for shirts and men's pants. Made in India and imported, Madras cloth was a staple fabric for men's shirts and women's dresses. These thread-dyed fabrics are difficult to date because the dyes and manufacture have not changed for centuries.

Ethnic tribal prints were increasingly used in clothing of the everyday United States culture in the years after 1960. Civil rights issues at home and the increasing global awareness of third-world countries helped influence the broader view.

President Kennedy proposed the idea of a man on the moon to the United States public. After his death, the idea continued with a well-funded space program. Rocket launches and updates kept the National Aeronautics and Space Administration in the public eye, and gave the world many new inventions, such as Mylar®. The first lunar landing occurred in 1969. Novelty prints related to rockets and stellar themes were in use during and after this time for little boys' rooms. Cowboy, firemen, and circus prints were also in use.

Selvage identifiers from manufacturers remained infrequent during the 1960s. Identifiers sometimes were as simple as plain, typewritten pica script along one edge of the fabric. Furnishing fabrics were more likely to have identification than dress or craft prints.

## QUILT STYLES

Traditional styles of the 1930s and 1940s continued to be followed in quilts, but there was an increase in the use of polyester fabrics. Kit quilts were still available and were virtually indistinguishable from the 1950s' era quilts, with the exception of a change in preferred batting. Polyester batting, sometimes referred to by its commercial name of Dacron®, was used after 1963. The appliqué kits still featured complexity ranging from beginner to intermediate skill level. Newspapers and magazines, such as *Grit, Women's Day,* and *Better Homes and Gardens,* carried advertisements for kit and pattern sales.

Artex International utilized ballpoint-tipped tubes of paint for colorizing preprinted designs on fabric. The items sold included pillowcases, sheets, hand towels, aprons, and quilt blocks, as well as the paints. These items have a distinctive stiffness. While some painters blended their colors, most left a distinctive, fine double stripe of color with a central lighter streak where the ball pushed the paint aside.

Embroidery or painting transfers could be purchased or self-drawn using transfer pencils. Purchased, preprinted blocks for thread embroidery were available in five-and-dime and general stores, as well as through newspaper advertisements. Some transfer patterns were red and some were dark blue.

Piecing patterns for quilts were frequently simple, possibly due to the increase in new quilters who were teaching themselves to quilt either alone or from a book. The advantage of this situation provided for the innovation of new techniques.

The free-form individualism of the 1960s encouraged quilters and other artists to reach beyond the conventional. The basis of the art-quilt style developed with experimentation in textile arts.

Creative appliqué designs sometimes included unique made-up elements of scraps in whatever size they came in. Geometric shapes were arranged in interesting patterns and applied. Daisy shapes and other modernistic themes were used. Pictorial appliqués often depended on the imagination of the quilter and were used to add ornament to quilts and clothing.

Sunbonnet Sue remained popular for children's quilts, as did Double Wedding Ring quilts for marriage gifts. Many 1960s' quilts were tied. Known as comforts, they required little skill to make, and the ties covered piecing inaccuracies. Denim was a favorite for blue jeans, which were recycled into comforts.

The batting preference slowly changed from predominantly cotton to polyester/Dacron, with some quiltmakers staunchly defending the use of cotton, and others willing to try a new fiber. Early polyester batting was not bonded, so it shifted and separated if not tied or quilted closely enough. Open- and plain-weave fabrics often allowed for bearding, with the polyester fiber working its way through the cloth's tiny openings. Flannel sheeting was also in use as filler.

Polyester and poly-cotton blend fabrics had some problems in their development. Some were the victims of gas fading, which means they lost color very quickly. Others were very tender. The cotton fibers disintegrated in combination with the polyester, leaving shredded, open holes. Pilling, which is the formation of small tangled balls of fiber on the surface of fabrics, was often a problem with polyester and polyester-blend fabrics. Polyester or cotton-wrapped polyester threads sometimes cut fabrics along seam lines of piecing and appliqué, irreparably damaging quilts.

Many of the quilts of the late 1960s illustrated new and imaginative designs, but the taste in pattern and color have changed over the intervening years. Quilts of the late 1960s and early 1970s are seldom shown as illustrations in books or magazines on quilt history. Few 1960s' quilts come out to be seen; many have been disposed of due to poor condition. Many 1960-era quilts are preserved for their sentimental value, not for pleasing aesthetics.

## QUILTED CLOTHING

In the 1960s, patched clothing became a fashion statement. In addition to the patching of durable blue jeans, quilt tops were recycled into clothing. Pieced clothing of random sections of prints were made. Old quilts were cut and sewn to make coats. Men's ties were remade into skirts, vests, and halter-tops.

Soft pink

Cotton – DayGlo® colors

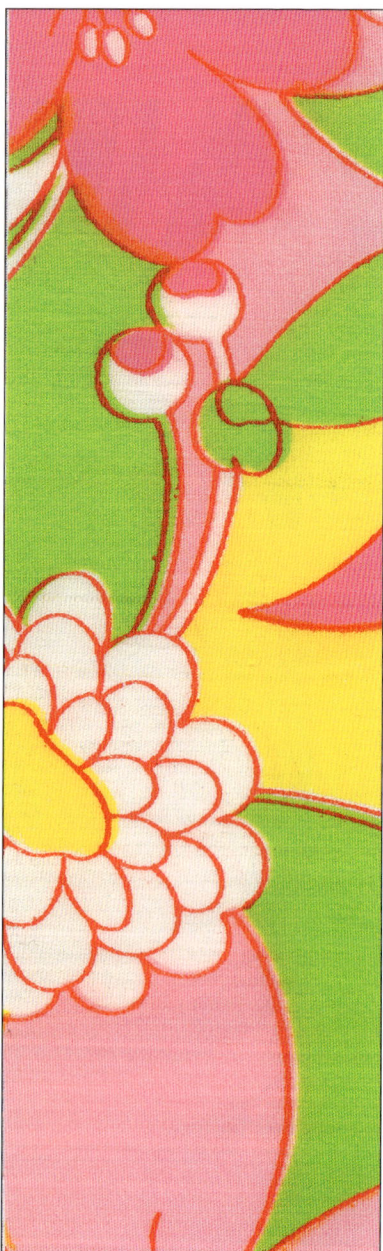

Bright green

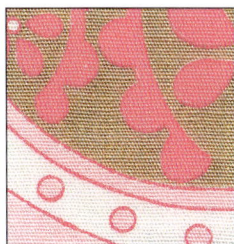

Bright colors in combinations

Bright colors, "mod" prints

Poly-cotton op art

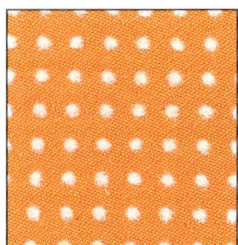

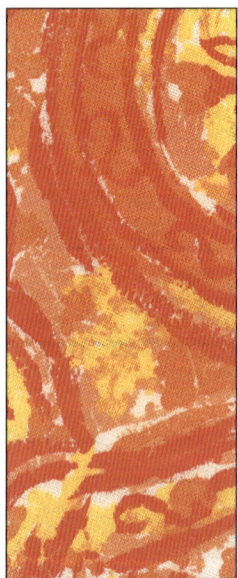

Orange, pink, and green combination

Bright colors
Lower piece: Hawaiian

DayGlo® colors

Large-scale cotton sateen

Black ground

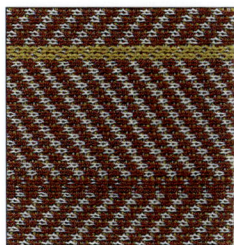

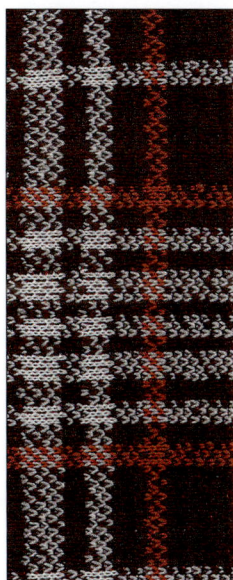

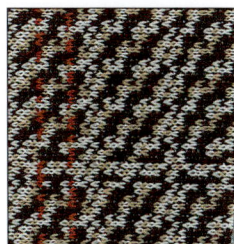

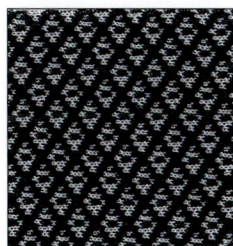

Polyester double knit and knit jersey
1960–1979

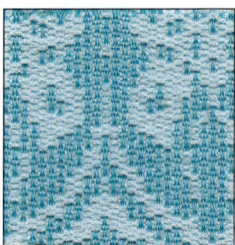

Polyester double knit
1960–1979

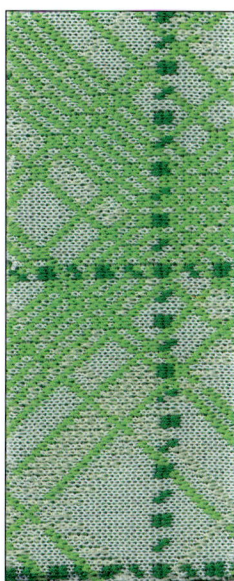

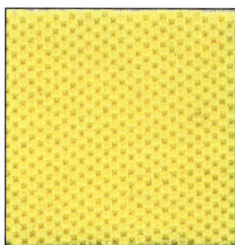

Polyester double knit
1960–1979

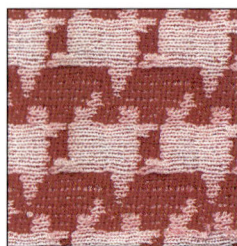

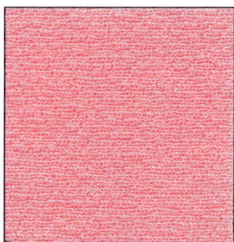

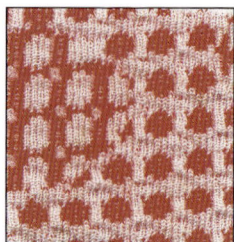

Polyester double knit
1960–1979
Lower right: swimsuit knit

# Bicentennial Revival

## ABOUT THE PERIOD

President Richard Nixon resigned from office and Gerald Ford presided over the bicentennial year in the United States. Jimmy Carter won the next election.

Partly due to the oil embargo of 1972–1973, an economic recession resulted in the lack of new houses. Combined with an historical awareness through the bicentennial, the lack of housing encouraged people to renovate old buildings. Vintage house restorations and colonial-style decorating inspired women to make quilts and participate in the "Spirit of '76." Interest in historical accuracy encouraged the production of fabrics copying originals.

Quilting began the stage in its history often referred to as the Bicentennial Revival. The trickle of books and information on quiltmaking became a steady flow. In addition, the establishment of quilt shows and quilt organizations on the national level remained as long-term influences on the quilt world. Quilts went from private bed covers to public works of art.

The National Quilting Association (NQA) held its first show at Greenbelt, Maryland, in September 1970. International Quilt Festival was first held in 1974, in Houston, Texas. Welcoming the retail aspect of quilting, it was an offshoot of the formerly successful wholesale Quilt Market.

The first Quilt National was held in 1979 at the Dairy Barn gallery in Athens, Ohio. The quilts shown were exclusively contemporary art quilts. Quilt National continued to showcase quilt artists whose vision was not limited by the traditional methods or materials of the day.

The bicentennial revival not only occurred in the United States, quilting was revived across the world. One of the most influential occurrences in quilt history was the importation of razor-sharp circular tungsten-steel blades into the United States in 1979. For the next 20 years, rotary cutters, self-healing cutting mats, and sturdy acrylic rulers revolutionized methods and speed of cutting, sewing, and producing quilts like no other items have.

## TEXTILE COLORS

Bright colors of green, blue, red, brown, and bright yellow were standards for little calico prints of the 1970s. Polyester and poly-cotton blend fabrics responded well to the dyes used, and saturated color was the result. Strong contrast of color was useful for black-and-white illustrations in books and magazines, as well as the few color prints used in publications.

# 1974 – 1979

The preoccupation in the 1970s with colonial themes also inspired a more subdued palette, imitating natural dyes. Shades of brown, green, olive, avocado, orange or peach, and warm golden yellow were used to give the patina of age to decorating schemes and quilts.

The American bicentennial inspired a patriotic surge of red, white, and blue color schemes, which persisted from 1974 through the end of the century. The brightness of the late 1970s' greens and reds is an outstanding feature of many prints. Purple was not a popular color choice for most 1970s' quilts.

## FABRIC STYLES

Many of the fabrics used in quilts of the era were a combination of cotton and polyester, or 100 percent polyester. Quilters of the era recall the difficulties of finding 100 percent cotton fabric for use in their projects.

Multitudes of small, tossed calicoes and ginghams were used in scrap quilts of the 1970s and the early 1980s. Country cozy, as promoted by Laura Ashley® and Jessica McClintock's Gunne Sax, showed floral influences and feminine styles.

Imported hand block-printed cottons and copies made in the style are evident in quilts, and were sewn into women's dresses and skirts. Stripes of varied widths were also popular in fabrics of the era. These were used for shirting, dresses, and both women's and men's pants. Heavy cotton canvas prints, often in printed or woven stripes or nautical motifs, can be found in 1970s' quilts.

One-color prints on a cream ground or the reverse can be found in 1970-era fabrics. They were relatively inexpensive to produce, and during the recession, cost-saving methods were important. They were also good for publishing purposes in magazines because they could be clearly seen in black-and-white photos.

Bandanna prints in bright red, medium bright blue, lemon yellow, teal, green, or orange with traditional black-and-white motifs were available. Gingham came in every color imaginable, but could be cotton, polyester, or a blend.

Sunbonnet Sue and Dutch Girl themes from the early 1900s served as design inspiration for Strawberry Shortcake®, Holly Hobbie®, and other big-bonneted whimsical girls promoted by American Greetings. These printed motifs often showed girls on plain grounds in random placement standing in tufts of grass or flower gardens, performing household chores or children's games. Scale varied from ½" to 12" figures printed on poly-cotton sheeting.

Imitation patchwork, referred to in quilting circles as "cheater cloth," was made of cotton, poly-cotton, or knitted fabrics and was popular for clothing and household decor. The color schemes were often in red, white, and blue; brown tones similar to the colors of the 1860 to 1870 era; or bright primary colors. Cheater cloth motifs often included rickrack designs and pictorial motifs. Prints were notorious for their poor registration accuracy. Companion fabrics utilizing the patterns shown in individual "patches" were also made in full yardage or with coordinated pillow panels.

Corporations were well represented, as cartoon spokesmen became part of the common culture. Sports teams, with their corporate status and ever-enthusiastic fan base, produced fabrics printed with team logos and mascots.

Scrap and sample packs advertised in the *Quilter's Newsletter Magazine* of the 1970s specifically stated that the sample packs would contain no knits – a clue to the prevalent fashion for double knit, knit jersey, and sweater knits available by the yard. While the knitted sweater cloth rarely made an appearance in quilts, the cross-medium influences are evident in some of the prints of the era. Double-knit fabric was used to make utility quilts (see pages 61–64).

Selvage identification by manufacturers became more frequent, but by no means universal. Designer fabrics for furnishings occasionally included the designer name on the selvage. The length of a fabric repeat could be measured from mark to mark along the selvage, and space was left in print fabric edges for selvage marks to be seen.

## QUILT STYLES

In the 1970s, books on the subject of making quilts proliferated. Some of these books extolled the virtues of tradition. Other books encouraged quilt-makers to use their designing talents on quilts for walls, beds, and bodies that were far from the established and accepted practice. Quiltmakers were encouraged to experiment with non-traditional materials, including such items as upholstery fabrics, paper, and plastic. In addition, beads, buttons, and found items were incorporated into innovative quilts.

More emphasis was placed on the accuracy of piecing. Pasteboard was being replaced with translucent plastic, which could be hand cut, and acrylic templates that were sturdy, neither of which wore down at the corners quickly. Until the 1970s varied seam allowances were used for quiltmaking, but directions in 1970-decade magazines and classes established a standard of $\frac{1}{4}''$ seams. Accuracy became as important an issue as pattern and color.

Fabric shops and continuing-education programs across the country offered classes to those who wanted the skills and social outlet provided by quiltmaking. These classes centered on sampler quilts that taught a variety of simple blocks. Sometimes a theme such as stars or flowers was chosen. Samplers made from color-coordinated fabrics and featuring large pieced blocks are a signature style of this era.

Polyester double-knit quilts appeared in this decade. Simple squares, rectangles, or half-square triangles were the most common shapes, though an occasional brave soul attempted more intricate piecing. Most are tied and may have polyester batting or flannel sheeting as the filler. The colors are normally bright, and the quilt is durable and often heavy. These double-knit quilts replaced the creation of most wool suiting sample quilts. Men's casual suits of the time were polyester leisure suits.

Satin acetate was used for wholecloth boudoir quilts in the era from 1930 to 1950, as seen in the movies. Satin acetate quilts were also made from 1975 to 1985, but generally were pieced of smaller blocks, sometimes as samplers. Acetate quilts were often the victims of gas fading, in which atmospheric gasses react with the fibers to create a change in color. Blues faded to purple and gray. Rose and pinks faded to orange. Bright yellows faded to butter color.

Appliqué designs were frequently simple, and sometimes were adapted from children's coloring books. Some designs were secured with a simple zigzag, and some with a satin stitch by machine. Nylon lace and embroidered embellishments were frequent. Appliqué sampler commemorative quilts were popular, with each block a pictorial motif representing some point in history. Many were made to commemorate the bicentennial.

Creative, original-design patriotic quilts were made for the bicentennial, and usually featured eagles, flags, and stars. Many red, white, and blue quilts that did not display a United States history theme were designed. Some were sold as kits. The bicentennial logo was sold as a limited-edition kit quilt motif for appliqué between 1974 and 1976, and polyester fabrics made these motifs difficult to apply.

Quilt series in magazines often featured embroidery outline designs, with each block a variant on a theme. State flowers and birds continued to be well liked, but new designs were also available. These designs were easily reproduced and not dependent on accuracy of sizing, like piecing patterns. Embroidery embellishment for creative appliqué was also common. Most featured simple stitches such as outline, French knot, and lazy daisy.

Kit quilts in the same patterns as those from 1940 to 1950 were still available through catalog sales and newspaper advertisements. The color placement remained the same, though some of the shades of solid fabric differed between the 1950 and 1970 decades. The small calico prints used in some of the kits differed very little during these years.

Many books advocated the use of flannel sheeting or Dacron batting for fill. Descriptions of cotton as being "difficult to quilt" and "mats terribly when washed" discouraged the use of it as filler. Backing fabrics were often poly-cotton sheets of floral or striped pattern. The batting for 1970s' quilts was frequently polyester, some presenting severe bearding problems. High-loft battings were frequently used, and the stitching was sometimes relatively large. Cotton batting was also used for many quilts. The use of wool batting was uncommon.

Quilting patterns of the 1970s depended heavily on straight-line patterns and outline quilting, stitched approximately ¼" away from the seam lines or appliqué edges. Some feathered motifs were occasionally used. Single, double, or triple cable twists filled sashing and borders. Quilting in general was minimal – one of the advantages of the new polyester battings was the greater allowable distance between quilting lines. Separation in batting after use was frequent. The often touted, high-loft batting forced hand stitches to be larger than thin cotton batting required. Machine quilting was sometimes used, but hand quilting was more frequently seen. Pictorial quilts and samplers required creative quilting solutions, or simple background fill.

A standard method of finishing edges was to roll the back to the front and apply it to the surface. Machine zigzag was employed occasionally for this purpose, but quiltmakers were also sewing the edges by hand. Separate bindings, either bias or straight grain, were applied to some quilts, but were usually only one layer of fabric.

The introduction of waterbeds and king-sized beds changed the requirements for some bed quilt sizes. Waterbeds were promoted with commercially made pieced velour bedspreads with polyester high loft batting. These were industrially machine quilted, in meandering lines. As these were used and washed, the nap frequently wore off, leaving the knitted fabric base exposed.

## QUILTED CLOTHING

In the 1970s, several quilting books covered the subject of creative patchwork clothing. Appliqué was mentioned as being useful for repairing blue jeans, but quilting in clothing was not limited to utilitarian patching. Antique quilts were cut up for use in new coats and jackets.

Magazines featured directions for making pieced clothing, as well as the varied pieced purses, bags, toys, men's ties, and pillows. Large random squares of fabrics were used to make patchwork skirts. Maxi-length skirts made a fine canvas for hand or machine quilting, or for appliqué patterns. Crazy quilt and patchwork dresses made it to the runways of fashion design and the Academy Awards. Patchwork was so commonplace that it was used as everyday clothing costuming in television and the film industry. The style became so popular that imitation patchwork, or cheater cloth, became a standard print style in fashionable clothing and accessories. In turn, scraps of cheater cloth were cut and pieced back into quilts.

Seminole piecing and reverse appliqué mola designs were published in 1970-decade quilt magazines, and their influences can be seen in clothing styles of the period. In 1979, the strip-pieced vest was so popular at Quilt Market, that advertisements and directions for making these garments were published in several quilt magazines.

Bicentennial commemorative

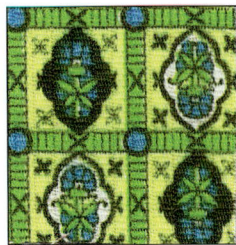

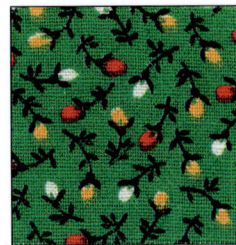

Green

Green

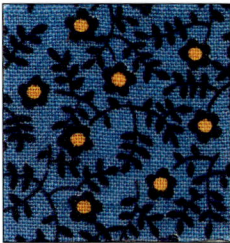

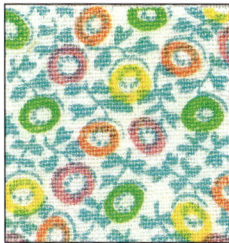

Light blue

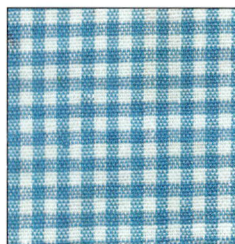

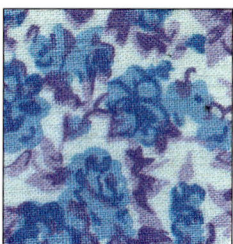

Light blue

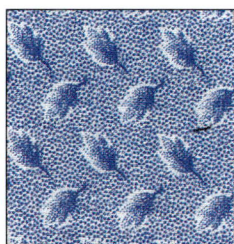

Light to medium blue, also chambray

Dark blue

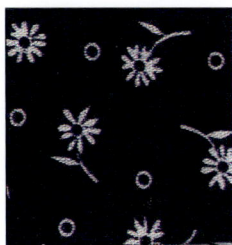

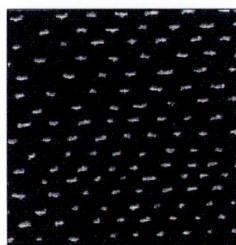

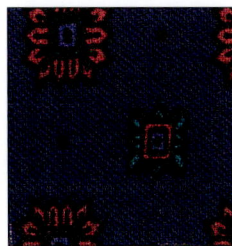

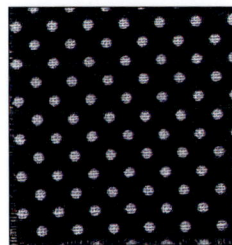

Dark blue, some on canvas

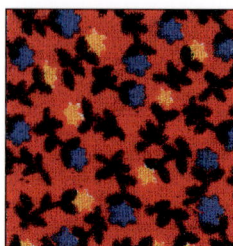

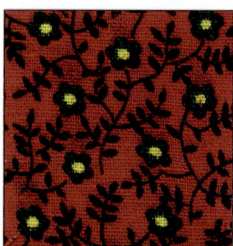

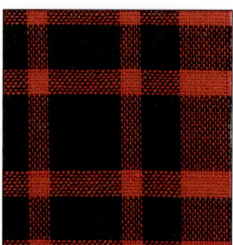

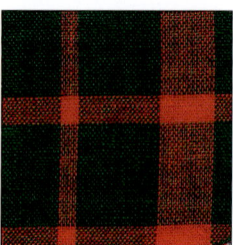

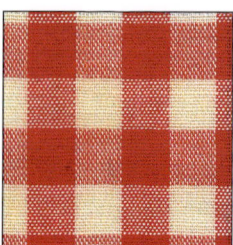

Dark red

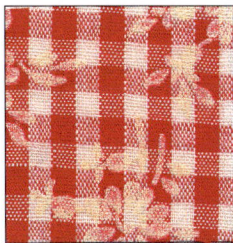

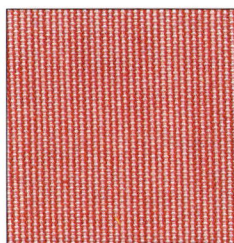

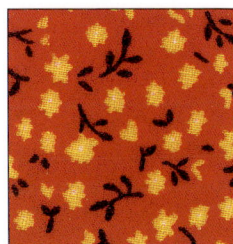

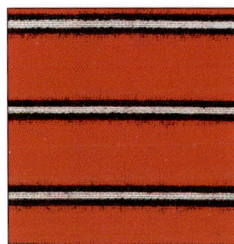

Bright red/orange

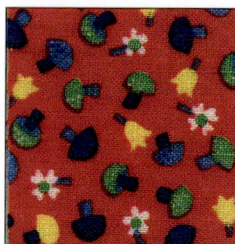

Bright red

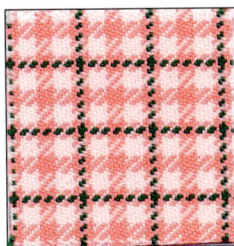

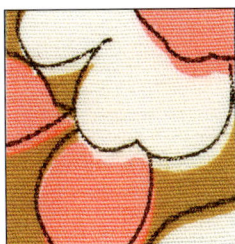

Soft pink to medium pink

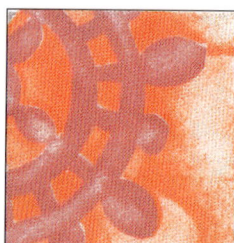

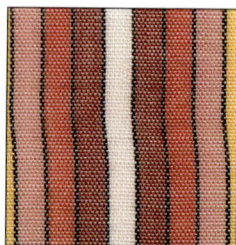

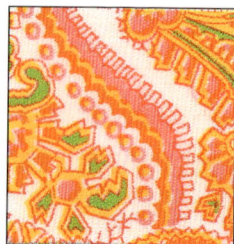

Pink with orange and dusky pink

Bright yellow to orange

Bright yellow to lemon yellow

Tan and sand-covered grounds

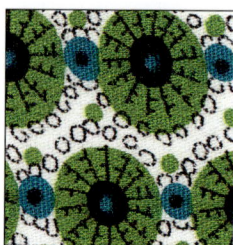

Light ground with green

*Dating Fabrics 2: A Color Guide 1950–2000*

Green and olive with rust tone

Beige, brown, olive, and light grounds

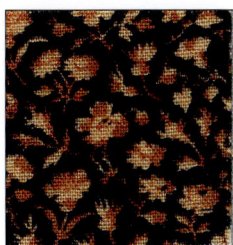

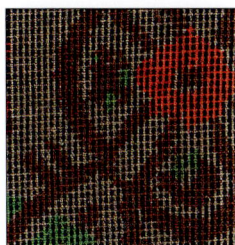

Dark brown and chocolate

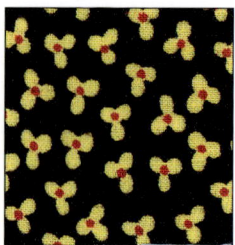

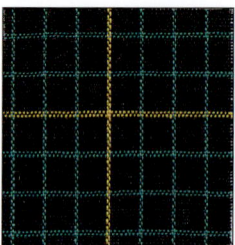

Black and black with brights

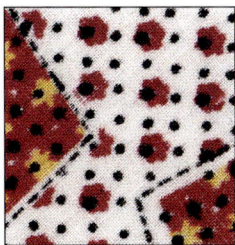

Preprinted patchwork – "cheater cloth"
Poly-cotton blends

Cathedral Window imitation patchwork
"cheater cloth"

Girls with big hats, poly-cotton blend
"cheater cloth"

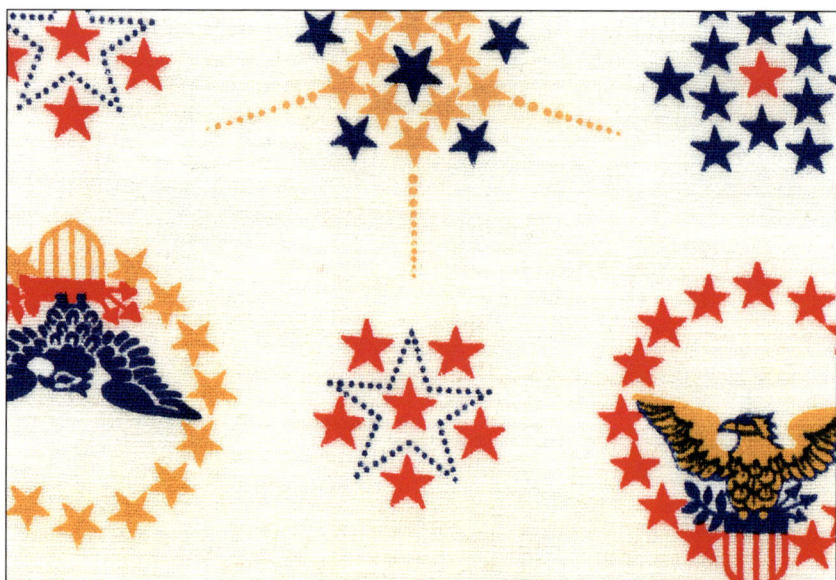

Bicentennial commemorative

Bicentennial commemorative, imitation patchwork
"cheater cloth"

# Material Girls and Guys

## ABOUT THE PERIOD

The presidential election of 1980 placed Ronald Reagan in office. The next eight years found a rising economy with more disposable income available for average Americans. As a result, both employed and non-employed women and men could invest in hobbies and their accouterments. In 1988, George Bush became the new president.

The 1980s also saw quilt-related occupations multiply, bringing many women into the business world. Teaching, writing, designing, and shop owner-ship gave women the opportunity to involve themselves with an activity they loved and a chance to earn money.

Quilt guilds grew more plentiful and active. They promoted interest in quilting through quilt shows, and introduced thousands of formerly uneducated consumers to the beauty of quilts. They challenged one another to be cre-ative, and were supportive of one another. They also informed one another about the latest new gadgets, encouraging additional sales for shop owners.

The American Quilt Study Group (AQSG) began in 1980 when a group of 50 textile historians met in Mill Valley, California. Since then, the annual confer-ence has increased the quality of historical scholarship in relation to quilts. Each year the publishing of the research papers presented in the journal *Uncoverings* made this information available to a wide audience. The Kentucky Quilt Project of 1981 was the first major quilt-documentation project in the United States. Thousands of quilts were photographed and recorded. It has served as a model for the documentation projects held in almost every state since then.

In 1985, the American Quilter's Society (AQS) held its first annual quilt show in Paducah, Kentucky, with an attendance of around 5,000. There were nine categories, including amateur and professional divisions. Award moneys were given, including some purchase prizes. In the first year, entries included quilts from Canada and Japan. In 1989, the first machine-quilted quilt to win Best of Show at AQS was CORONA #2: SOLAR ECLIPSE by Caryl Bryer Fallert.

Many quilters of the 1960s and onward came to the quilting world not as sewers or clothing makers, but from arts backgrounds. In 1986, *Quilt Digest Press* publisher Michael Kile and quilt historian Penny McMorris presented the traveling exhibit, The Art Quilt. In 1988, the first biennial exhibit of innova-tive art quilts, known as Visions, was sponsored by Quilt San Diego. A pictorial catalog has been produced for each exhibit to commemorate these shows and expose the idea of quilts as an art form to the general public.

The rotary cutter had become better known throughout the 1980s. New rulers were developed to use with the rotary cutter, which made for faster and more accurate cutting and piecing. The late 1980s saw a new phenomenon – home computers. Personal computers allowed quilters to communicate in groups, which facilitated the development of Internet quilt guilds.

## TEXTILE COLORS

Unlike fabrics made from 1920 to 1950, which were frequently produced in one or two opposing shades on the color wheel, fabrics from 1980 and later exhibited a wide variety of colors and shades in one print. Fabric lines featured a lead fabric that included color variety and companions that harmonized with one or more of the lead shades. Many 1920s' to early 1970s' prints had two to four colors in a single print. By the late 1980s, up to 17 colors could be used in a single print. The introduction of computer-control improvements to the rotary screen-printing process allowed faster printing with more accuracy.

Favored color combinations in home décor heavily influenced the selection of quilt fabric in the early to mid-1980s. Traditional-style quilts frequently featured soft hues in coordinating tones, but toward the end of the decade, darker colors in the same type of combinations ensued. Wedgewood blue and peach from the early decade became navy and rust. Powder blue and pink became medium blue and dark rose. Mint tones and peach morphed into teal and rust by the 1990s. Lilac or lavender and butter yellow in the early 1980s became violet and gold by the end of the decade.

Hand-dyed fabrics provided a complete range of color. If you could not purchase the color you wanted in fabric, you could make it yourself. By the end of the decade, to capture the market, fabric manufacturers were producing almost as wide a range of solid colors as could be hand dyed.

Op-art black-and-white prints were frequently used in dramatic ways for quilts of the art genre. These could also be overdyed to subdue the high contrast. Studies suggesting that infants and children were favorably stimulated by the use of bright colors and black-and-white prints encouraged the use of these color schemes in quilts. Primary colors were in use during the entire decade. By the late 1980s, hot colors such as neon green, hot pink, and chartreuse were back in favor.

## FABRIC STYLES

At the beginning of the 1980s, tiny floral calico prints were heavily promoted for use in quilts. These were used along with commercially produced solid fabrics for many quilts. In 1982, representatives from Hoffman Fabrics attended Quilt Market, and found quilters eager for the elegant florals and paisleys for which Hoffman Fabrics has become famous.

In the mid-1980s, Ely & Walker, a division of the St. Louis-based dry goods supplier, discontinued production of cotton fabrics after over 100 years of business. Many of its patterns included small calico types, which were going out of fashion. By the late 1980s, "reads as solid" prints were available, especially those that provided texture without the closely packed floral motif that had been popular for so long. Throughout the 1980s and 1990s, the scale of floral prints used in quilts again expanded.

Tropical prints, such as those used in Hawaiian shirts and appliqué quilts, were available in quilt shops, especially once they were promoted for their subtle shading and selective cutting possibilities. Border stripes made lovely frames for quilts and blocks and interesting selective cutting possibilities. Large-scale paisley prints were also used for selective cutting and alternate setting blocks.

Fiber-reactive dyes were sold commercially by 1956. By the 1970s, they could be purchased in quantity by the small-scale dyer. Many home-based companies developed in the early 1980s. Dyers strove for solid colors with no variation, which required constant agitation of fabric in the dye bath.

Step gradations, a varied intensity of selected hues, were a popular special effect. At first, unblemished tones were desired, but crinkle-dyed fabrics were much less labor intensive and produced many different print effects. Both color styles were sold in quilt shops and at quilt shows by the mid 1980s.

Other fabrics that could be dyed in the home studio or purchased from specialty dyers were marbleized and shibori resist-dyed. Visual clues for dating these specialty fabrics are presently unclear because a home dyer could use any plain cloth available for purchase, and these unusual effects were used from the 1980s to the present.

Ethnic prints, such as wax-resist prints from Dutch Java and batik from Bali, were imported to the United States. The Javanese wax-resist prints were sometimes produced on fabrics with a semi-coarse weave, which could ravel easily. Bali batik was usually hand painted or resist-dyed and overdyed onto fine-weave pima cotton or rayon. Both looks were copied in American fabric designs on cotton. Heavily glazed and colorful Kinte cloth from Africa was also imported, and imitations were soon available.

Tissue lamé, made from the metallic-appearing Mylar®, which was developed for the space program in the 1970s, was a way to add sparkle to quilts in the 1980s. This fabric was frequently backed with fusible knit or plain-weave cotton for stability in quiltmaking. The polyester metallic fibers were very sensitive to heat and ironing. Lamé that was cleaned or treated with inappropriate chemicals could melt or discolor. Metallic jersey knit was also used in quilts, but the surface abraded easily.

Manufacturers' selvage identifications became evermore frequent with increasing amounts of information added. Depending on the fabric line, one could have discovered the designer, manufacturer, copyright date, how many colors were used, and whether the print was properly registered. Manufacturers developed individual signatures for their company, so a small portion of the mark could identify the company by the style of text in the selvage.

An increasing variety of choice, the tendency of fabric companies to discontinue fabrics lines faster than before, shorter bolt "put ups," and the desire to have a full palette of colors for whatever the next project might be turned many quilters into fabric collectors.

## QUILT STYLES

Throughout the 1980s, the relationship between the clothing people wore and fabrics used for quiltmaking became more distant. Inexpensive, everyday clothing made overseas and sold through national chain stores was often unsuitable for quiltmaking. Imported clothing provided no leftover scraps for the quiltmaker to use.

Series classes in quilt shops and continuing education programs taught a variety of quiltmaking techniques, resulting in sampler quilts. Color-coordinated quilts, suitable to match decorating schemes, were popular. Most sampler quilts are included in this category because classes usually included lessons on choosing colors. A common method taught for fabric selection was that of choosing a large-scale multicolored print, and a variety of companion fabrics in colors to coordinate. These were often assembled in the "quilt-as-you-go" style. Magazine articles featured theme series, influencing a number of similar but not identical quilts. Quilters would then purchase their own fabrics to recreate the example.

Wholecloth quilt kits were available in the 1980s. Pre-marked wholecloth nylon tricot was advertised for quilting, but was rarely seen. Preprinted cotton tops for wholecloth quilting were frequently finished with a different backing fabric, though matching fabric was available. Improvements in ink made it easier to remove the preprinted quilting lines than on earlier quilt kits. When quilters designed their own wholecloth quilts, the tendency was to have the top and back of matching fabric; the penciled quilting designs are sometimes still evident.

Quilts for children and adults utilizing simplistic appliqué were promoted in magazines of the early 1980s. These were sold in pattern or kit form, which could be found nationwide using the same groups of fabrics for the pieces. Kits for pieced and appliqué kits were available. Many of the kit quilts remained the same as those promoted for the previous 40 years. Embroidered kits of blocks and full quilts could be purchased through craft stores and catalogs, and were usually printed on poly-cotton fabrics.

A fascination with the Amish lifestyle and the presentation of their quilts as graphic art inspired a number of imitation quilts in the Amish style. The

Amish, on the other hand, began to make quilts for sale to tourists that contained printed fabric, including formerly forbidden appliqué.

The rotary cutter may have inspired the number of strata quilts, made from strips and strings and sometimes pieced on a foundation by the flip-and-sew method, a technique formerly utilized for Log Cabin quilts. This method was used to make optical landscape quilts, in which sections of strata were cut and pieced into an abstract design. Bargello-style strip-pieced quilts were being taught in classes and entered in quilt shows by the late 1980s.

In 1987, family members of AIDS victims created "quilts" to commemorate their loss. Known as the NAMES Project, these quilts or panels featured the name of the deceased and articles of special remembrance by their family and friends. Some of the panels were quilted and some were not because most of the makers were not originally quiltmakers. To display, the quilt panels were laid out on the ground or floor, side by side in sections, much like oversized quilt blocks. Walking paths between the panels resembled sashing.

The first public showing of NAMES quilts was on the mall of the United States capitol in Washington DC on October 11, 1987. The exhibition began with 1,920 panels. By October 2001, at the end of a year of touring, the NAMES Project included over 44,000 panels, representing 82,000 deaths due to AIDS. It has been recognized as the largest community arts project in the world, and more panels are being made all the time.

Miniature quilts had the appearance of full-sized quilts, but were made to fit a standard, small scale of proportion. Small quilts were also being made, but to differentiate from miniature, they were not made to fit a standard reduction scale. Rubber-stamped fabric or paper flip-and-sew patterns made intricate small piecing possible.

Pictorial quilts, featuring figures and/or scenery, became evermore popular. One could remember a trip or create a representative idea through the use of pictorial piecing or appliqué. Pictorial quilts of the 1980s often feature small calico prints or solid colors.

Nontraditional quilts often relied on plain solids for their special effects. Many book and magazine illustrations of the early and mid-1980s utilized these colors, first commercially produced, and later hand dyed. Experimentation with the illusion of depth and transparency took place and was created with color placement in design, utilizing both commercial and hand-dyed fabrics to achieve the desired effects. As the decade progressed, more effective illusions of depth were shown, as the blending of art and quilt became more practiced and pronounced.

Challenge quilts were more of a group project, with one or more theme fabrics chosen, and a group of participants choosing to represent an idea in cloth that featured the theme fabrics. Nationwide challenges, such as that sponsored by Hoffman Fabrics, inspired even more friendly competition.

American quilts from the early 1980s show a predominance of polyester battings, with more frequent use of cotton battings toward the end of the decade. Some cotton battings caused spotting on the quilt surface from flecks of cotton plant impurities left in the batting. This was mostly resolved by the end of the 1980s. Quilting at greater intervals was possible when battings with a foundation scrim were used. Wool batting was available but rarely used, and usually needed cheesecloth to help prevent bearding.

Quilting amounts were usually minimal. Straight-line designs and ¼" outlines were the main quilting elements at the decade's beginning. Fill patterns for alternates were often feathered wreaths, circles, baskets, or grids, but most outer areas of plain blocks were left unfilled. Patterns from the 1930s were still available and in use. In the early 1980s, quilting stencils were changing format from pasteboard or posterboard to plastic. Painting stencils were sometimes used to mark quilts. Often, only the drawn lines were quilted because quilters failed to connect the stitches where the bars support the stencils.

The introduction of the washout blue marking pens and fade-away purple pens had mixed reviews. The blue pen could become permanent depending on the rinse water, and some quilters did not completely rinse away the marker, leaving ink in the batting that would rise to the surface later. Purple pens faded away during dry seasons, but could return when the humidity was high.

Bindings were usually bias cut from a fabric coordinating with the quilt, applied by machine to the top of the quilt, then hand applied to the back. By the end of the decade, double-layer bindings, referred to as Double French, were the norm. Quilts made for children and charity often did not have applied binding, but were sewn and turned in an envelope style.

Poly-cotton sheets, especially those that had a high thread count, were often difficult to quilt through. While grandma knew enough to look for a certain thread count, books rarely mentioned this as a criterion for choosing backing sheets. The use of sheets for backing quilts rapidly fell out of favor. Quilters increasingly backed their quilts with printed cotton, cut in lengths and sewn together to fit. Print backings of 100 percent cotton were being sold in wide widths especially for quilters by the late 1980s. During this time, quilters were discovering how poor stitching on the back could be hidden by small-scale busy prints.

With the frequency of quilt shows increasing, many muslin hanging sleeves were added to the top edge of quilts. By the 1990s, these were often planned as part of the quilt, made of fabric to match the back lining, and sewn into the binding. In the 1980s, quilt groups and historians began promoting the labeling of quilts, listing the maker's name and date of completion, size, quilt title, and perhaps the reason for making the quilt. These labels indicate the crossing over of quilts into the art field, and also the prevalence of competitive quilt showings. The identifying information may be inked or embroidered.

## QUILTED CLOTHING

Many quiltmakers purchased patterns to make piecework jumpers, especially using homespun or coarse-weave plaids, and reproduction country-style prints. Newly pieced fabrics were used to create bomber-style jackets, with zippers up the front and knit cuffs and collars.

Seminole piecing was a late 1800s' technique of cutting and re-piecing solid-color fabric strips, and the addition of rickrack trim. The assimilation of the style into the popular quilting culture was facilitated by the rotary cutter. Seminole piecing found common usage in jackets and dresses in the 1980s, and later served as inspiration for the "row" quilts of the late 1990s.

Early 1980s' quiltmakers sometimes made their first experimental quilt blocks into projects such as tote bags, book covers, and vest backs. Large blocks were often pieced into denim or canvas for bags.

The Fairfield Fashion Show inspired quilters and clothing makers alike. It was an eagerly awaited event at the Houston Quilt Market each fall, and showcased the talents of internationally known quiltmakers and quilted wearable artists. Few things were too far over the top for these concept clothing pieces. The Hobbs Bonded Fibers Fashion Show debuted at the American Quilter's Society Quilt Show & Contest in Paducah, Kentucky. Clothing shown there was usually of a more wearable type, and perhaps encouraged clothing makers to see themselves wearing quilted garments.

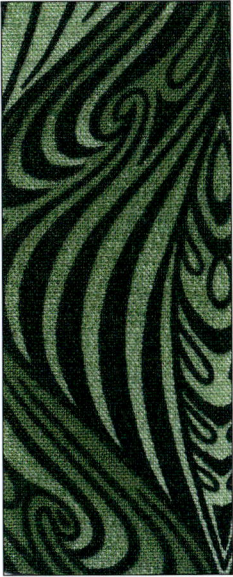

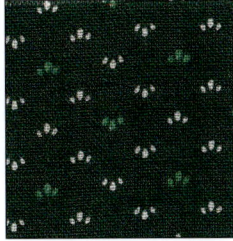

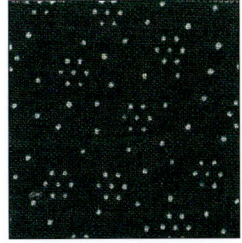

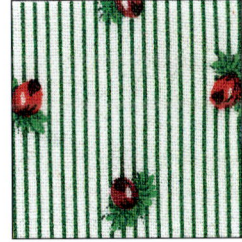

Dark green

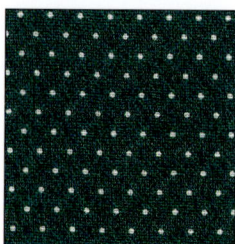

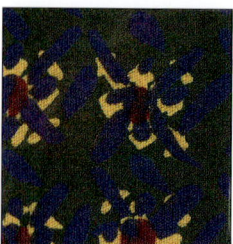

Dark green

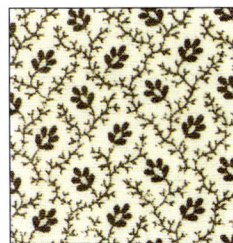

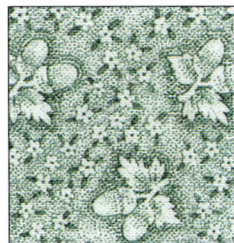

Medium to light green

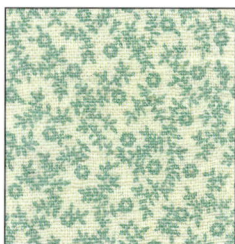

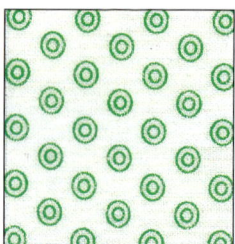

Mint to dark green

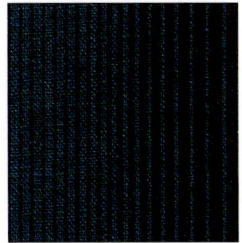

Dark teal

Medium blue, light blue, and teal,
some with white overprints

Navy blue,
some reproductions, some homespun-type

Bo Bo Dima,
wax resist and indigo
from Dutch Java

Varied purples

Varied-scale purples, light tones

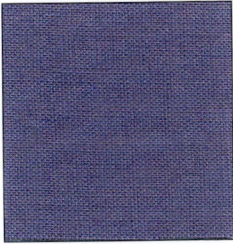

Dark purple tones,
some "read as solid," some reproductions

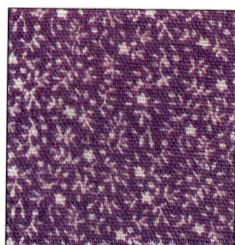

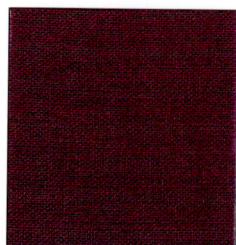

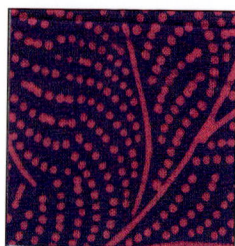

Dark rose to magenta

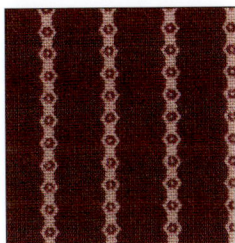

Light burgundy,
some reproductions

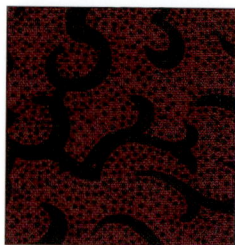

Border stripe, dark burgundy

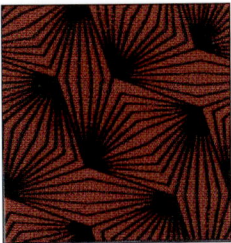

Red with black or navy
Lower right: gold overprint

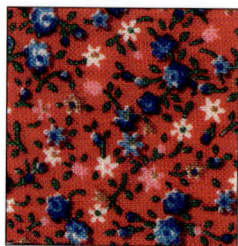

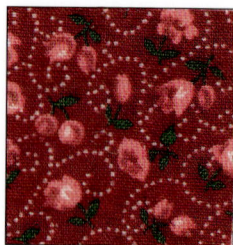

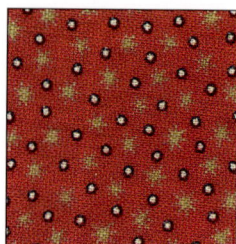

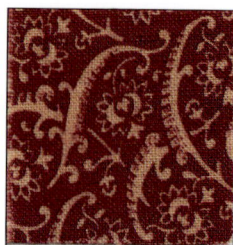

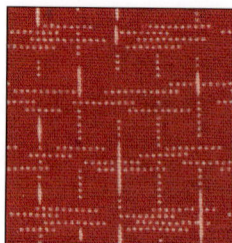

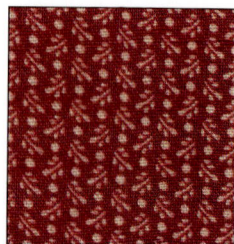

Cranberry to red,
calico novelty and reproductions

Dark red

Large elegant paisley

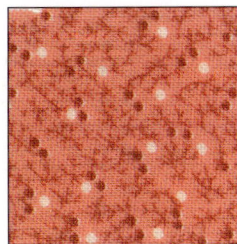

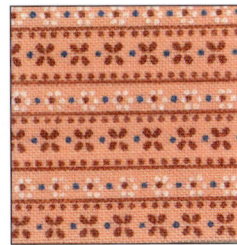

Peach to rust

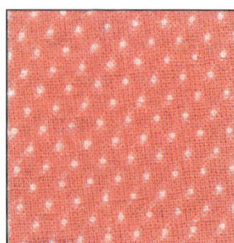

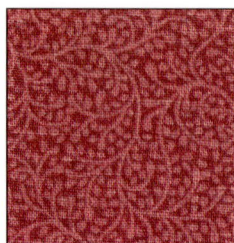

Rose pink

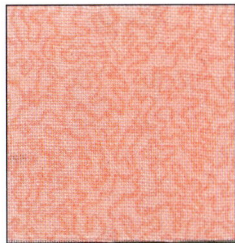

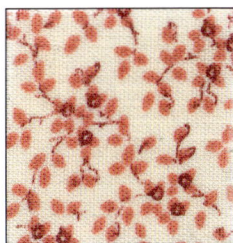

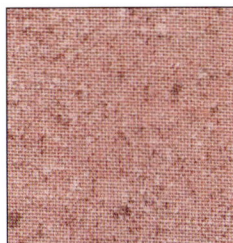

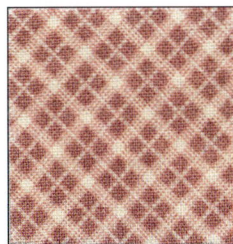

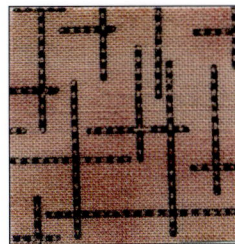

Dusty pink

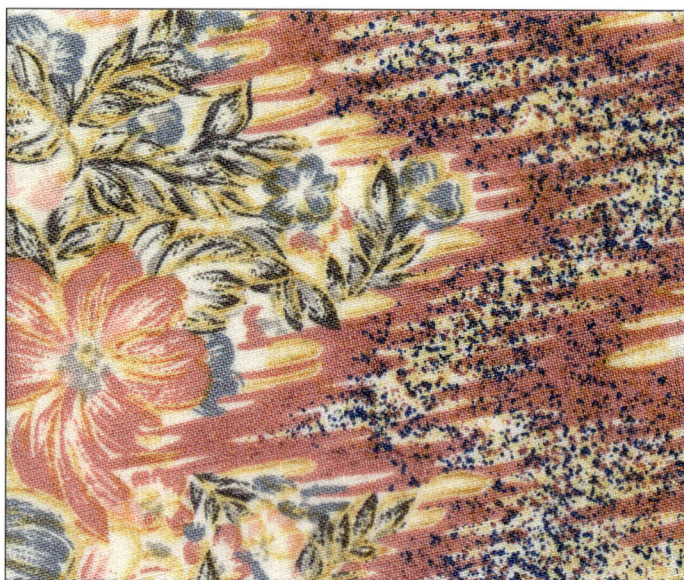

Scattered floral with grounds

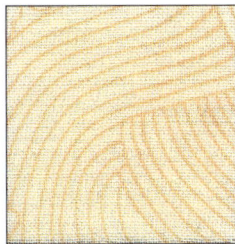

Yellow to yellow gold

Cream to yellow

Top and center: brown to tan
Bottom: glazed chintz

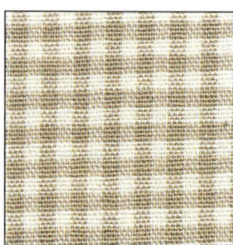

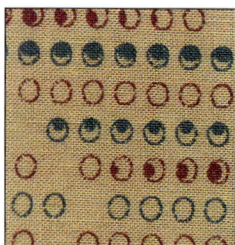

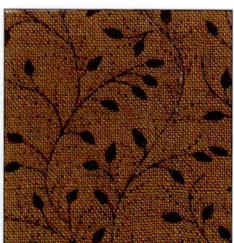

Beige to brown

Dark brown/chocolate

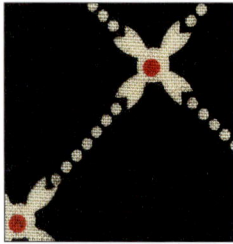

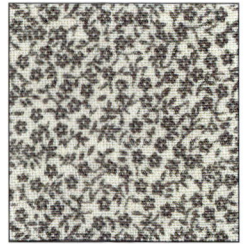

Black with accent, gray

Photoprint quilt collage

Holiday theme
Lower left: photo print

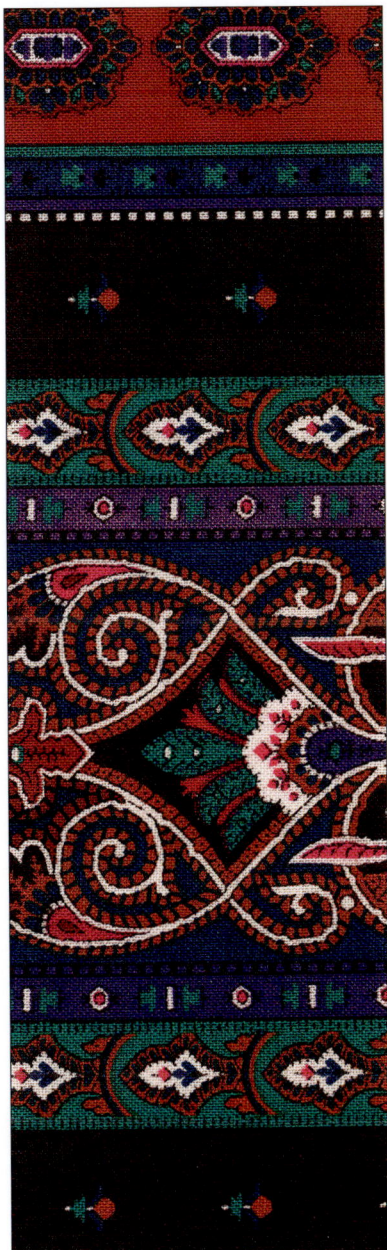

Border stripe

# *Anything Goes*

## ABOUT THE PERIOD

George H. W. Bush was in office when Iraq invaded Kuwait. America sent its army to defend Kuwait, and force Iraq to withdraw. Norman Schwarzkopf and Colin Powell became war heroes. The Gulf War inspired many patriotic quilts as quiltmakers used the long-familiar medium to voice their support and concerns. William Clinton was elected president in 1992 and served two terms.

The concept of quilts as art or craft continued to be examined as the two sides blended, each learning and influencing the other. Traditionalists studied color theory and its use in quiltmaking. Art quilters continued experimentation with shape and form so basic to traditional quilts.

Quilt shows drew greater numbers of participants and attendees from all over the world. Ideas were traded worldwide and quilters often shared their materials with new friends overseas, which was aided by the Internet, job placement of expatriates and military families, and friendships formed at quilt shows.

In 1991, the Museum of the American Quilter's Society opened in Paducah, Kentucky. It soon featured changing exhibits plus selections from the permanent collection, as well as quiltmaking classes. As a response to the Smithsonian licensing agreement to reproduce American quilts overseas for sale to support museum needs, the Alliance for American Quilts began in 1993.

The prevalence of the personal computer, and the increasing capability of the machine and the user, changed the way quilters could plan their new quilts. Computer-aided drafting programs made it easy to plan original designs, place fabric, and even calculate the yardage needed for a project. Such programs did not always work as a timesaving device, but allowed the planning of virtual quilts that may never come to fruition in reality.

One major element of home pattern design and production was continued dialog into copyright infringement, public domain, and public use. Many quilters who were part of groups had the habit of sharing patterns they purchased, and copying magazine articles for each other to share. Designers and publishers, who depended on sales for their livelihood, disapproved of this practice and were sometimes willing to take matters to court to prove their point.

## TEXTILE COLORS

While a particular shade may have been difficult to find for a season or two, the 1990s found quilters with a full spectrum of fabric colors available in the store or in their stash. With the rapid changeover in fabric lines and the desire for widely divergent prints by an ever-increasing number of quilters, no fabric requirement went unsatisfied for long. The tendency of quiltmakers to stockpile a hoard of fabrics, fondly referred to as a stash, made certain that desired colors would be available for a long time.

Reproduction fabrics and tea-dyed looks filled the niche for fabrics with brown overtones. Reproductions of the 1920s and 1930s and a variety of soft pastel companions filled a need for a softer look. Quilters bemoaned the lack of yellow choices in earlier years, but the late 1990s made up for it with wide varieties of yellow, orange, and gold. Its opposite on the color wheel, purple, grew evermore prevalent during the decade.

Bright electric colors in tropical prints and juvenile themes with companion fabrics were available. These hot colors were printed on dark grounds or used for strong contrasts with black backgrounds. Some of the black backgrounds were black-on-black prints, providing texture and depth.

Many of the white, off-white, cream, or muslin fabrics were printed with white patterns, adding texture and depth to the backgrounds of appliqué blocks. Some of these overprints were a thick resin base, and were difficult to hand quilt.

## FABRIC STYLES

Much of the cotton fabric for the craft trade was printed overseas, especially in Japan and Korea. Some influencing factors included reduced labor costs, quality of production, and in some instances, Environmental Protection Act restrictions on the use of dyes within the United States.

Fabric manufacturers found ways to keep quilters buying. They shortened print runs and stopped repeat production of patterns. New designs were constantly being introduced. Bolts of fabric were prepared in shorter "put ups" so shops were not purchasing large quantities that might not sell. Fabric turnover was faster. Quilters with extra spending money learned to become impulse buyers for fear that a fabric might sell out.

Quiltmakers of the 1990s tended to make quilts in the colors they desired, but not necessarily those that would fit a specific décor. They made quilts for friends and family based on themes and favorite color choices, as opposed to the narrow parameters of decorator design. Large- and small-scale novelty prints were available to commemorate the owner's favorite animals, occupation, food, or fantasy. They could be serious or comical theme prints.

Fabric for almost any holiday celebration, including St. Patrick's Day, Halloween, Christmas, Hanukkah, and Kwanzaa, were available. If you tried hard enough, you might have even found fabric for the fictional St. Urho's Day, with purple grapes and mustard yellow.

The 1990s was a sparkling decade. Gold, silver, and copper metallic over-prints enhancing color cotton ground prints were available for use in any season. These are most often found on paisley prints, stellar or constellation prints, and elegant holiday-theme fabrics. Silver and gold also embellished creams, whites, and pastels. Resin-bonded glitter prints were available, but tended to leave a trail of sparkle behind.

While tissue lamé was a signature of the 1980s, the difficulties of preparing it for use in quilts influenced quilters to look for other fabrics to add the sparkle they desired. Imported plaids and stripes from Thailand and India with a metallic Lurex thread were used in quilts and decorative pieced clothing. Metallic holographic transfers were available for use privately, but usually were not commercially available on cottons until after 2000. The early holographic prints were susceptible to damage by ironing.

Quilters did not limit themselves to the plain-weave cottons on the market. Many included rayons, silks, and upholstery fabrics in their quilts. Quilt clothing artists experimented with varied fibers, stabilizing fabrics when needed.

New companies that came into being in the 1990s were sure to include selvage identification, which had become a standard over the last decade. Fabric manufacturers included selvage identification on most of their craft fabric designer lines, at the insistence of the designers themselves. However, solid-colored fabrics, as well as those that were vat dyed and overprinted, were unlikely to have edge identification.

## QUILT STYLES

Attempting to describe the quilt styles of the 1990s and beyond seems like an exercise in futility. Anything one says could be considered too limiting. Instead of being comprehensive, this is a listing of some highlights.

Quilt styles of the 1990s covered the range of possible quilt styles. Some quilters were "purists," and insisted on hand-pieced and hand-quilted quilts, using only 100 percent cotton fabric. Other quilters were more adventuresome, and included almost every conceivable technique and material.

There was an increase in the use of hand appliqué for design motifs and an increased level of skill to perform it. Books from the 1980s by a variety of authors encouraged people to make the effort. Fusible underlining and sewn-in stabilizers took some of the fear out of machine appliqué.

Realistic pictorial themes such as those shown in album quilts and post-card quilts utilized the landscape fabrics and other creatively cut fabrics. Hand-dyed and painted or commercially produced sky fabrics were a perfect foil for rolling hills of trees and grasses. Pictorial quilts from the 1990s generally feature specially printed landscape theme fabrics, tailored to the pictorial market.

Paper-piecing techniques of the 1980s matured, and intricate piecing was made easier by the use of it. The predominance of long, narrow triangular points was supported by the use of paper foundations for accuracy. Mariner's Compass, Sunburst, Rocky Mountain Railroad, Crown of Thorns, and other varied pointy block patterns, once the domain of intrepid quilters, became commonplace in the late 1990s.

Selective cutting, also called fussy cutting, enhanced simple piecing and appliqué patterns, making them appear more complicated. At the end of the decade, Bethany Reynolds' Stack-n-Whack® and other kaleidoscope techniques taught quick methods of rotary-cutting repeat patterns out of large-scale prints.

The introduction of programmable embroidery machines for home use, and the possibilities for use of the home computer to create personal artistic designs which could be stitched with those machines, provided unique design opportunities. These embroidered designs were used as individual panels for embroidered sampler quilts and motifs to add to crazy quilts. Hand embroidery saw a revival in the form of redwork and bluework for blocks and bedroom accessories.

A crazy quilt revival in the 1990s and later was fed by the availability of multitudes of imported decorative ribbons, beads, buttons, charms, and other embellishments. This also encouraged the use of handwork for the embroidery and beadwork required to heavily embellish the quilts and other items in the "crazy" style. Books of stitchery techniques and ideas about how to use them were published. Color transfer techniques on fabric made photos of family and friends part of the crazy quilt genre. Art quilts were also often heavily embellished.

Quilts made from the color-transfer motifs on cotton knit T-shirts were a personal expression. These were usually stabilized with iron-on adhesive and cut into uniform sizes depending on the quilt. Simple sashing outlined the blocks, and the quilts were usually tied, because quilting through the iron-on transfer plastics was difficult by hand or machine.

The mid-1990s brought a variety of printed flannels into the quilting mainstream. Flannels were often in rustic tones, such as plaids, reproduction-style florals, and monotone prints. These were precursors to the flannels of the early 2000s, which covered every available range of color and print style.

Another type of quilt made in the mid-to-late 1990s was the rag quilt, in which seam allowances were left on the outside, then washed to fringe the edges. Sometimes, many layers of fabric were used to create extra-thick fringing, reminiscent of chenille bedspreads.

The ultimate charm quilts were made in the eve of the twenty-first century. Quilters planned and drafted designs to use either 2000 or 2001 different fabric pieces in one quilt top. These fabrics were sometimes traded over great distances, often internationally, aided by online chat groups devoted to the swapping of fabrics. Many millennium quilts feature one or more of the fabrics specifically created to commemorate the occasion.

Quilt backings were usually made of commercially produced cotton prints, sewn together to fit the required size. Some specifically made the center strip one width of fabric, and placed the narrower sections along the sides. Manufacturers were also making 100 percent cotton backing fabrics, related to their fabric lines, in wide widths for use in quiltmaking.

A phenomenon referred to as back art occurred in the late 1980s and early 1990s. This is creative piecing of fabric, usually closely related to the fabrics of the top, which creates a separate but complete secondary design. It may be difficult to determine which is the right side. The indicators include an applied sleeve of matching fabric along the top edge, or evidence of a label on the lower corners.

## QUILTED CLOTHING

The Fairfield and Hobbs Bonded Fibers Fashion shows helped inspire quilters to try their hand at creative wearables. Quilted clothing was more than a cut up old quilt to wrap about you. Creative piecing and seam lines in nontraditional placements made clothing into art to wear.

Quilted clothing could be worn with style and fashion in mind. Clothing was not limited to the use of cotton fabric. Silk and rayon lent themselves to flowing garments that were freeing, feminine, and graceful.

Dimensional effects through creative manipulations enhanced clothing in a multitude of ways. The addition of buttons in odd places, beadwork, and ribbon work all enhanced the effects. Multiple needlework, such as that for heirloom French sewing also served as embellishment.

Books on wearable art were sold in quilt shops and shows, sharing ideas on how to utilize creative ideas in clothing. These often included the same techniques that were in use for embellishing quilts, including tucking, silk ribbon work, appliqué, free-form machine embroidery, buttons, and beading.

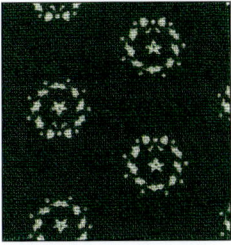

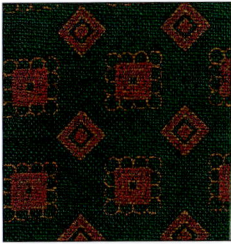

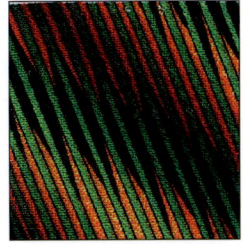

Greens, some with gold overprint

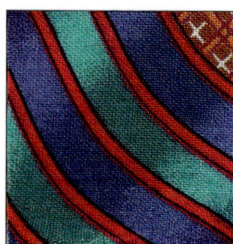

Dark teal
Center: realistic floral

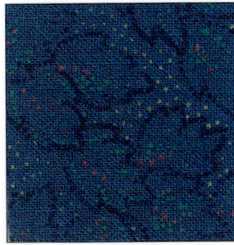

Dark teal
Center: art illusion print

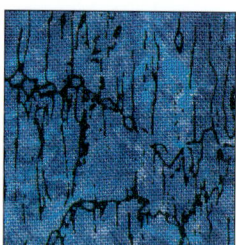

Dark blue, some with gold, some reproductions
Bottom: large leaf

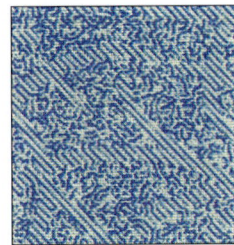

Medium blue

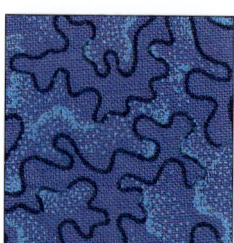

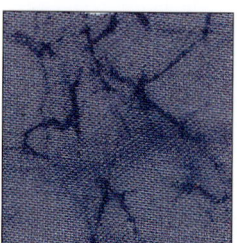

Medium dark to dark blue,
some reproductions

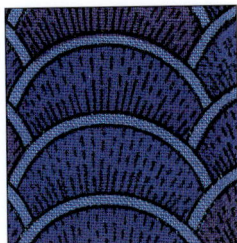

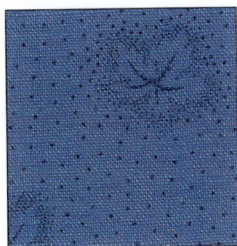

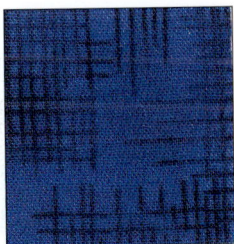

Medium to dark bright blue

Celestial prints

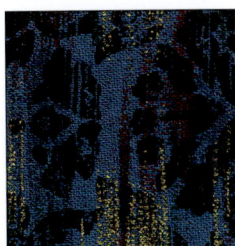

Metallic overlay on blue,
silver, or gold

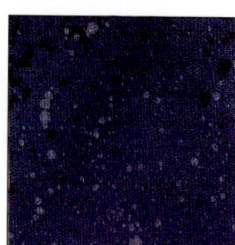

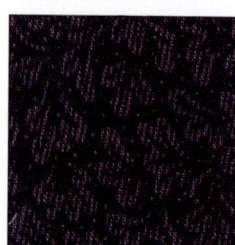

Dark purple,
some with gold overprint

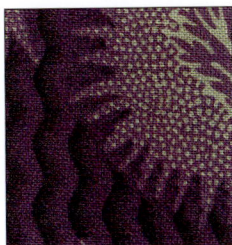

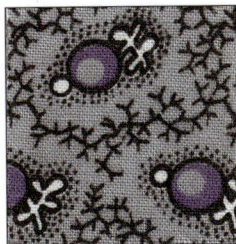

Dark to medium purple, some reproductions
Center: imitation Bo Bo Dima

Dark to light purple
Center: glitter frost

Medium-scale prints

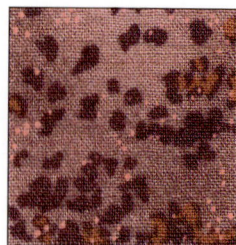

Purple
Left panel: shaded ombré print

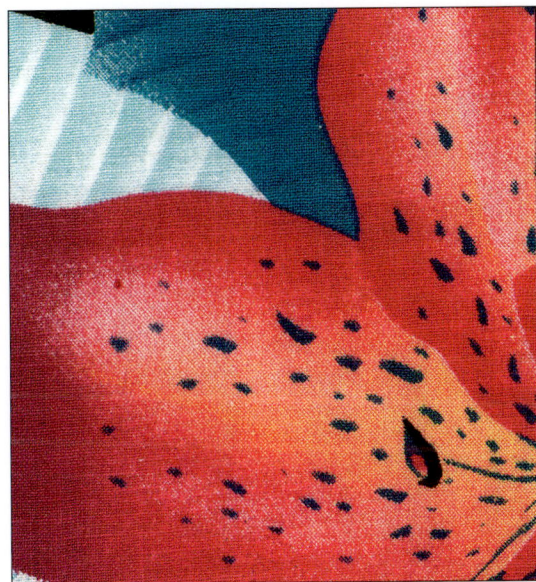

Fuchsia pink
Right panel: shaded ombré

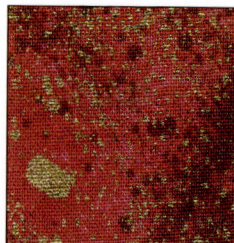

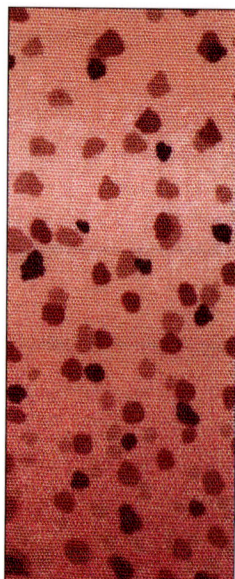

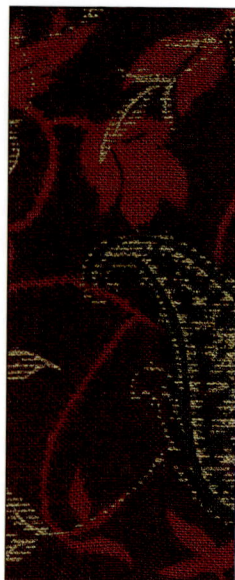

Dark rose to burgundy, some with gold overprint
Upper left: oriental influence

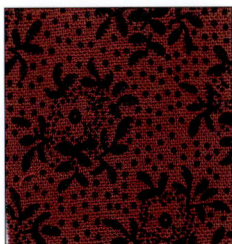

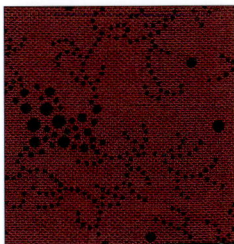

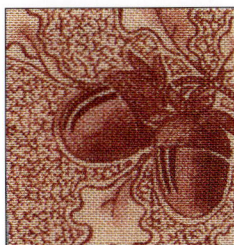

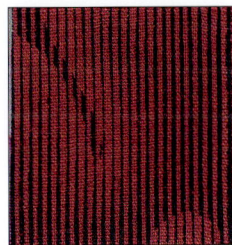

Dark burgundy

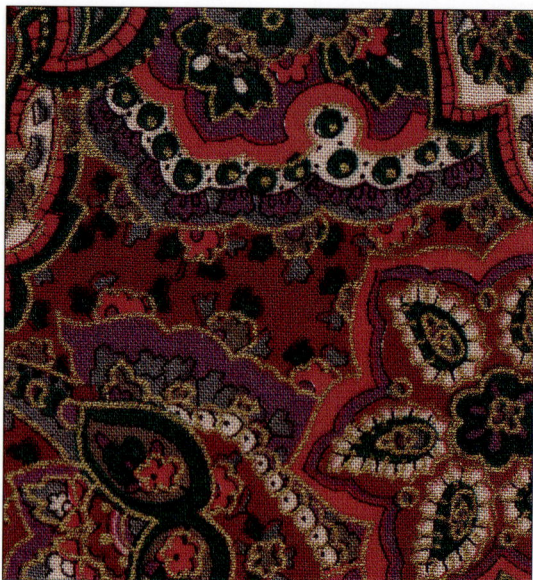

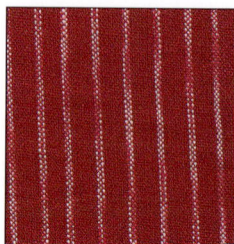

Dark red
Upper left: overall red rose print

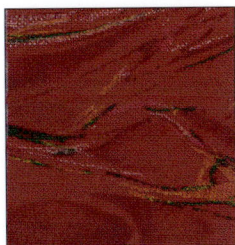

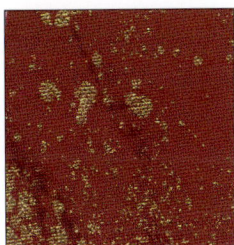

Dark red
Left panel: large-scale tropical

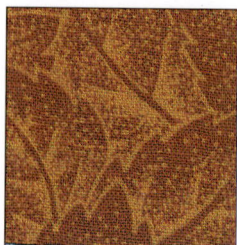

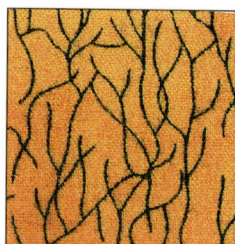

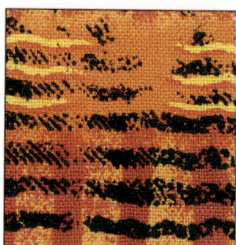

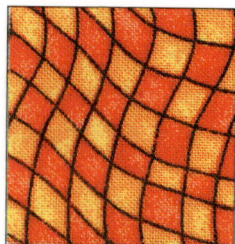

Orange to rust

Orange to rust, ombré shaded
Left panel: gold overprint stars
Right panel: celestial with gold overprint

Dark rust
Upper right: glitter frost

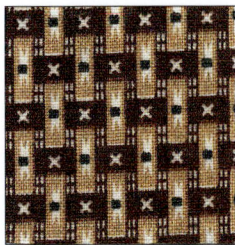

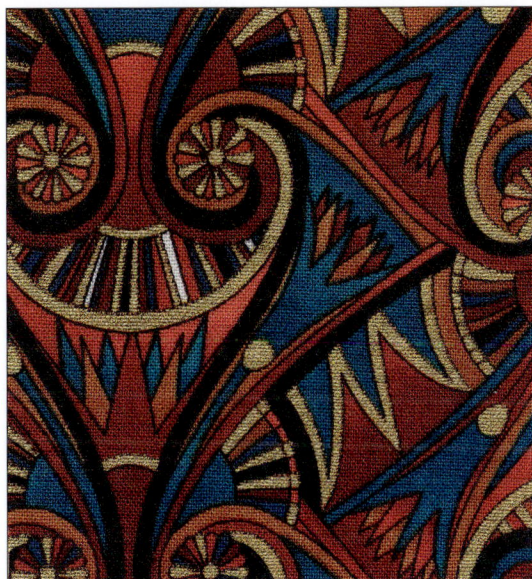

Dark brown

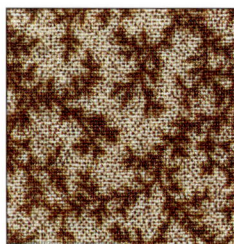

Beige to tan, novelty corn

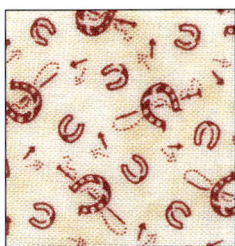

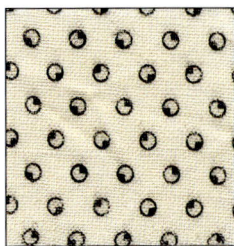
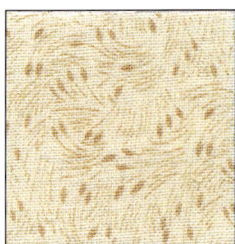

Light grounds,
shirting, conversationals, and *toile* floral

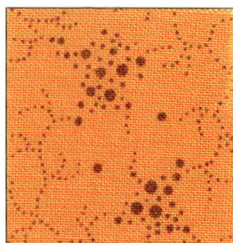

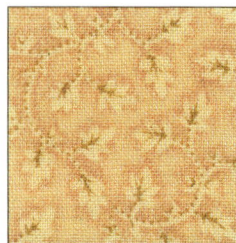

Yellow to "chrome" orange,
Upper left: oriental influence
Upper right: provincial influence

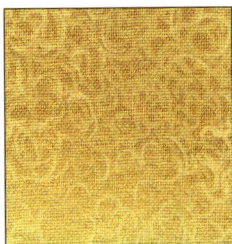

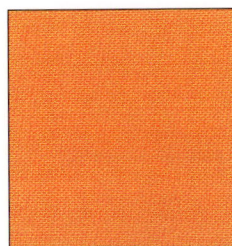

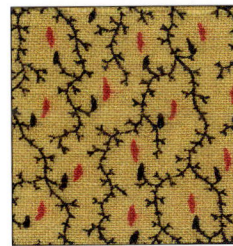

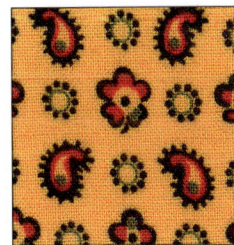

Yellow to orange,
including 1850–1930 reproduction styles

Large-scale tropical

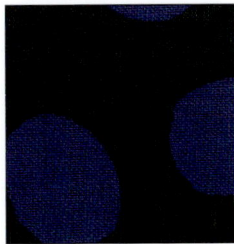

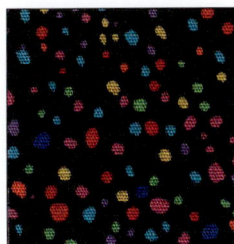

Black with brights

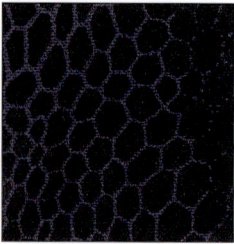

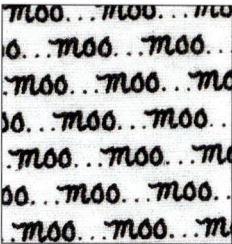

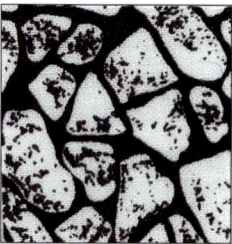

Textured black

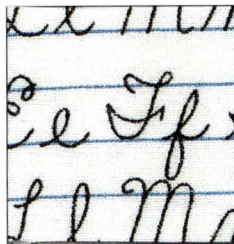

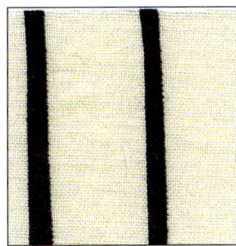

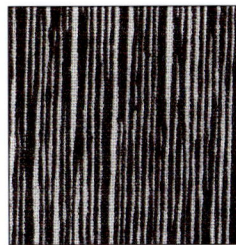

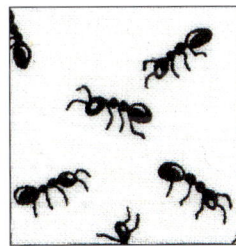

Black and white, sometimes overdyed

White on white or muslin, often overdyed, sometimes in steps

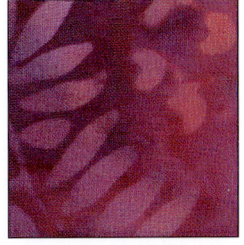

Batik – cotton or rayon

Batik – cotton or rayon

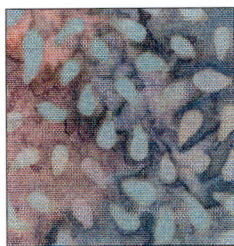

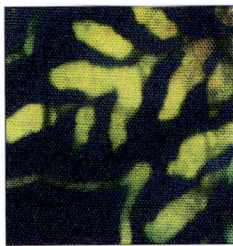

Batik – cotton or rayon

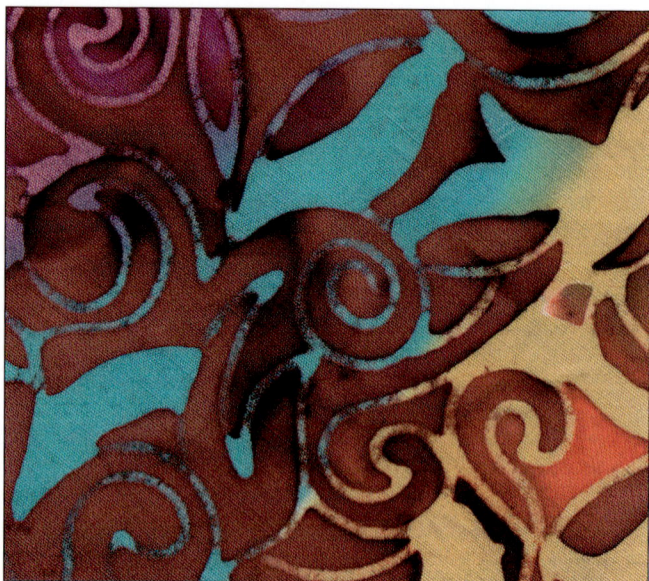

Batik – cotton or rayon

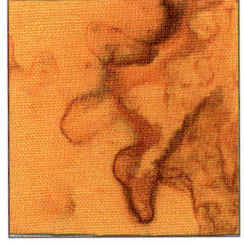

Batik – cotton or rayon

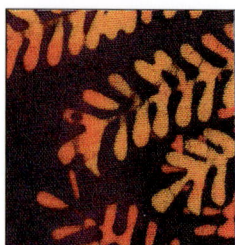

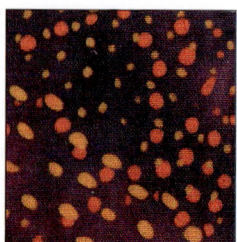

Batik – cotton or rayon

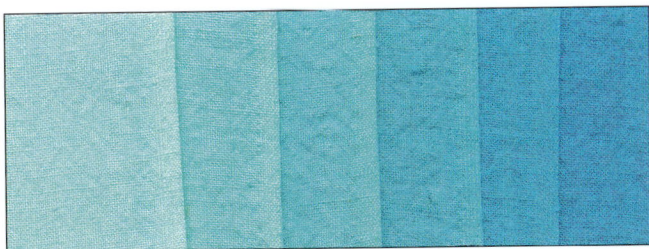

Six-step gradation, solids

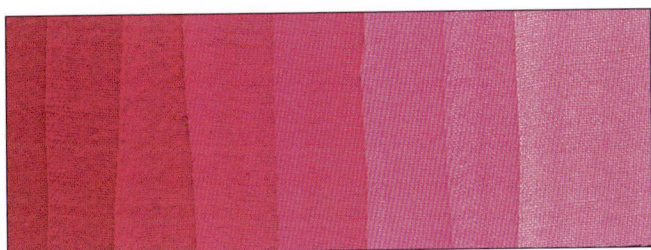

Eight-step gradation, solids

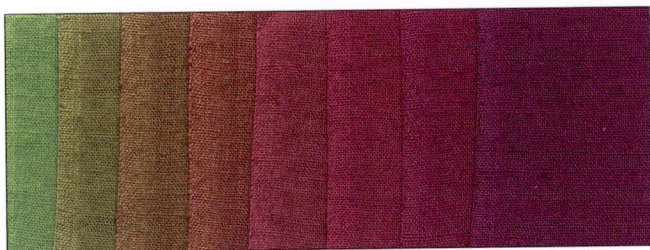

Eight-step gradation, tone to tone

Six-step hand-dyed krinkle

Hand-dyed krinkle

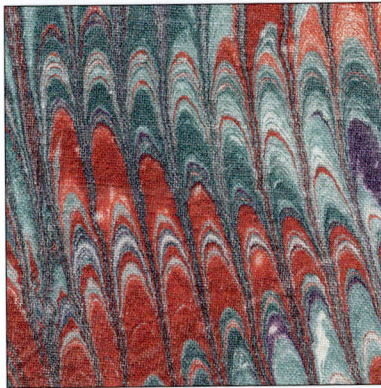

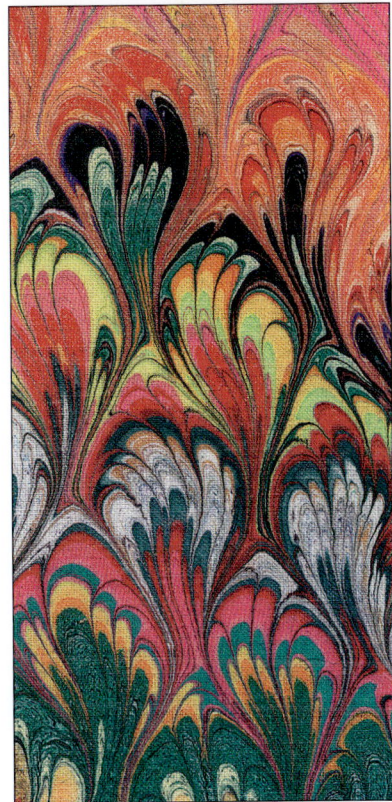

Hand-dyed marbleized

Wide border stripe

Scenic Native American novelty

Florals
Often used for colorwash quilts

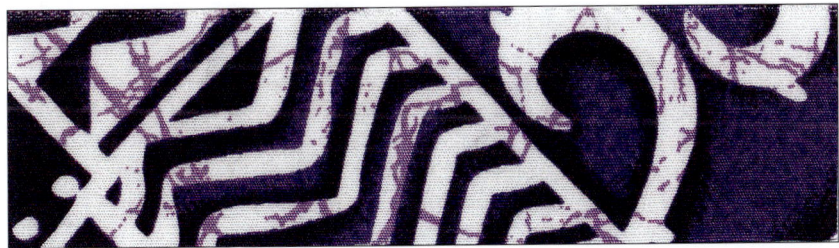

World cultures

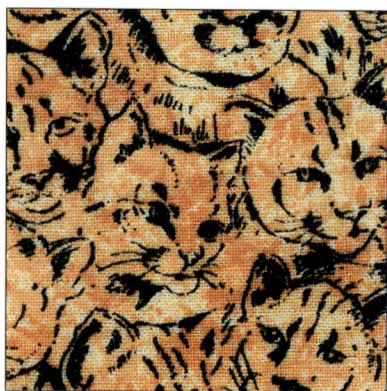

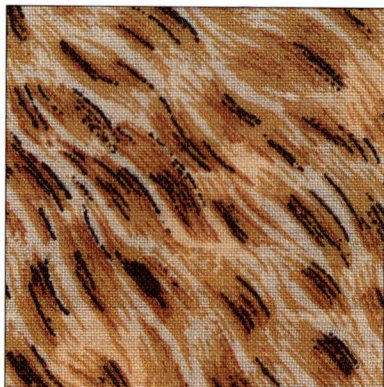

Cats novelty

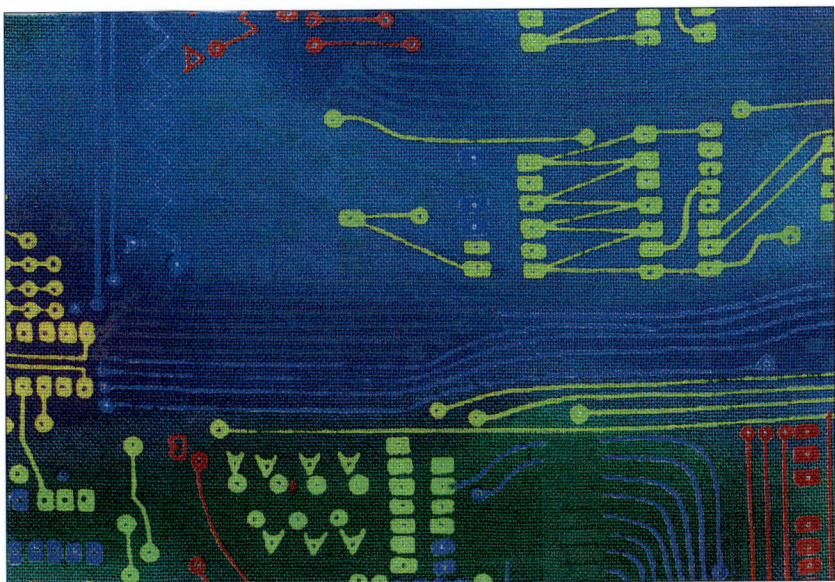

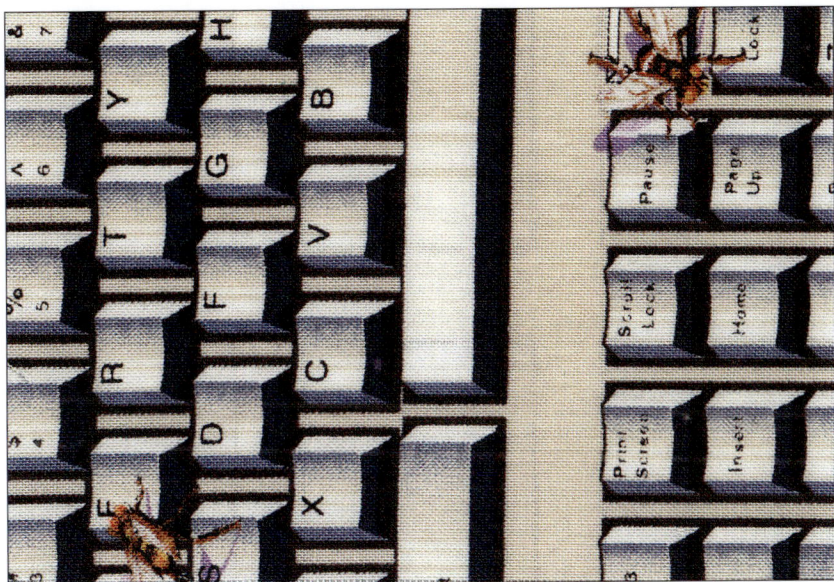

Computer-theme novelty

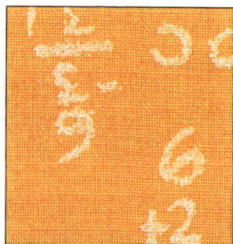

Music and school novelty

Bugs and butterflies novelty

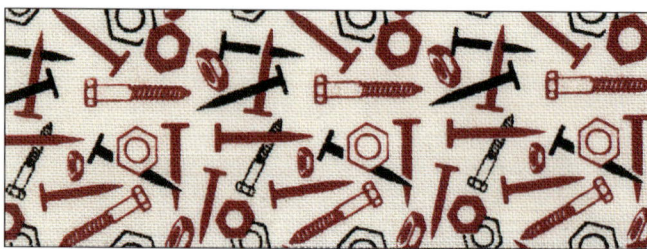

Tools, nuts, and bolts novelty

1492–1992 Columbus commemorative novelty

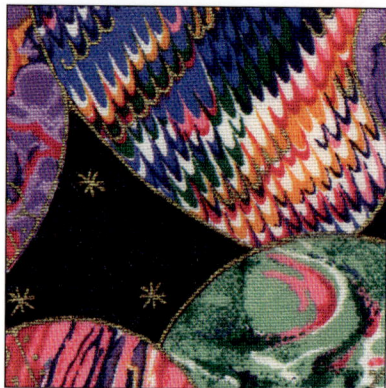

Holiday-theme novelty

Christmas novelty – rose pink

Christmas novelty

Christmas novelty – blue

Millennium 2000 commemorative novelty

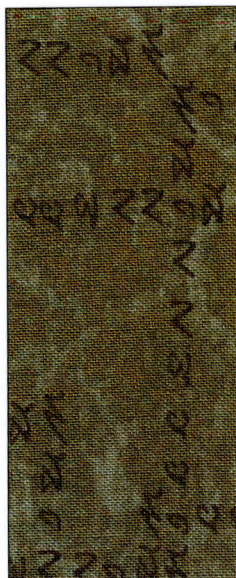

Millennium 2000 commemorative novelty

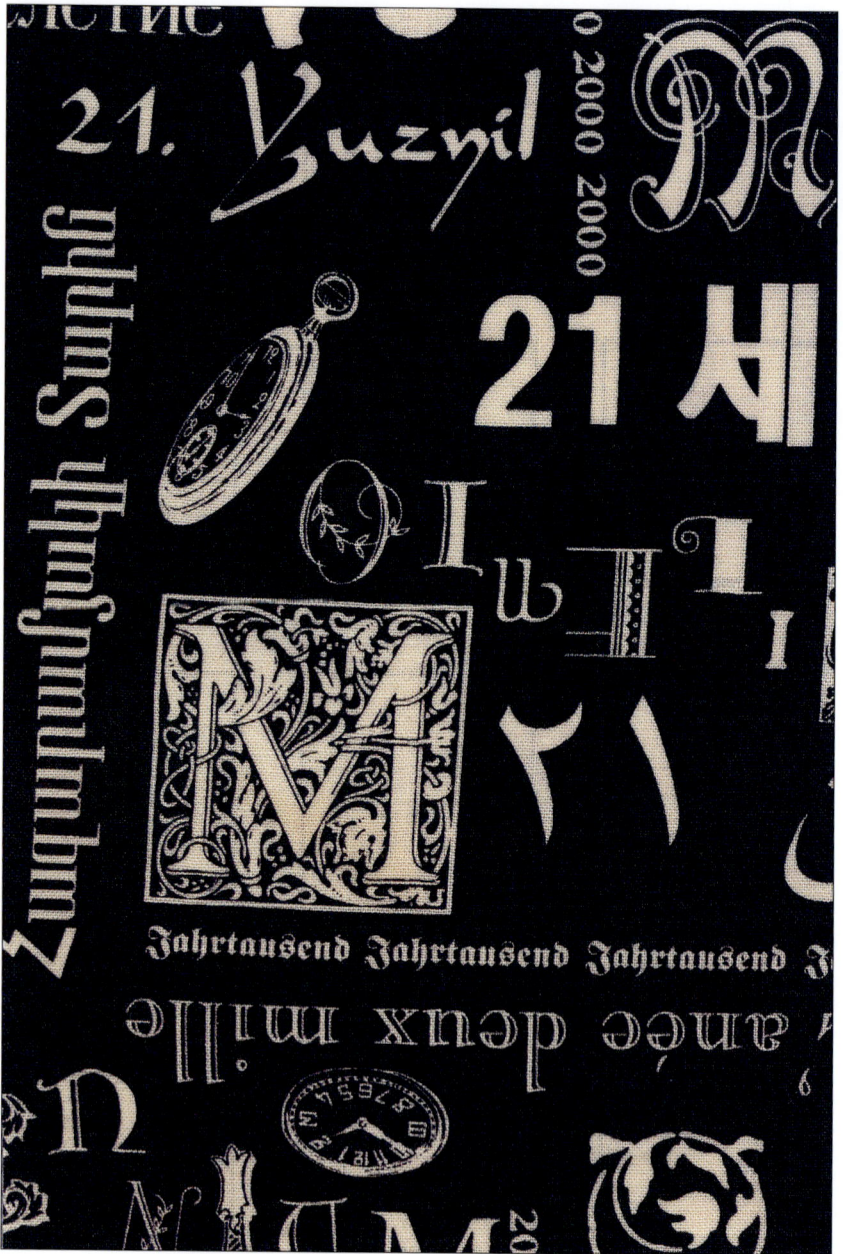

Millennium 2000 commemorative novelty

*Dating Fabrics 2: A Color Guide 1950–2000*

# *Reproduction Fabrics*

## WHAT GOES AROUND COMES AROUND

In recent years, the proliferation of reproduction fabrics has caused some concern among quilt collectors and quiltmakers regarding the ability to differentiate between old and new fabrics when used in quiltmaking, reproduction quilts, and repairs.

Fabric design lines come and go quickly. Most have a limited production life, but may remain on the shelves of quilt shops for many years. In addition to distinctly named reproduction fabrics, many other fabric lines are close copies of older print styles, in period-appropriate colors. However, modern fabric companies like to have a full line of colors, and will often produce a reproduction in a color that is *not typical* of the time of the original print.

Many methods of treating quilts and fabrics to make reproduction fabrics appear older are available. After quilters turned to overdying with tea or Rit® dye, several manufacturers adopted brown tones in their fabric lines to create the look of old, used, dingy colors.

There are some points of comparison between authentic and reproduction fabrics that will not be changed by any form of manipulation. While extensive studies can be performed by reliable institutions to be absolutely certain, there are methods that the average person can also perform.

Counting threads per inch *has not* proven to be a reliable indicator of age. An examination of reproduction fabrics shows a range of thread counts between 65 and 80 in warp or weft threads per square inch. Antique fabric thread counts show the same varied range of numbers.

The first step to consider in comparing new and old fabrics is the twist of threads used to weave fabric. Warp and weft threads of fabric prior to 1930 are often of uneven thickness when viewed through a linen tester. While the difference may be minimal, it results in an uneven lie of the weave. The threads of new cotton fabrics are usually evenly twisted, resulting in a smoother, more even weave. The exceptions to this appearance are homespun plaid and stripe types that are made in centuries-old methods of spinning and weaving, which are still employed in some third-world counties.

Another helpful method is to examine a width of fabric from selvage to selvage, if it is available. Fabrics from the 1800s could range anywhere from 18" to 32" in width. Early 1900-era fabrics generally range from 22" to 36" in width. Many late 1900s' plain-weave cotton fabrics range from 41" to 46" in width, though the bolts generally state the width to be 44" or 45". Poly-cottons from the mid-1900s also fall into the 40" to 45" range. Silk bolts are generally 45" to 54" wide. There are always exceptions to these general guidelines.

Examining the wrong side of the fabric can also help determine age. For example, indigo blue fabrics have been available for centuries, the color has long been loved by quiltmakers, and many antique quilts utilized indigo fabrics. Therefore, many manufacturers provide reproduction indigo-type prints. An examination of 12 randomly selected discharge-printed indigo blues of the 1880–1900 period showed no more than 60 threads per inch. The thread weave was not very even because the thickness of warp and weft threads varied greatly within the fabrics themselves. While all of the vintage pieces had blue backs, the white-resist pattern was visible through the cloth, but not completely. The vintage fabrics were easily frayed, and ones that had been washed had a soft, flexible texture.

Recent imports of indigo-dyed fabrics show the same print indications of vintage fabrics. They are correctly termed remanufactured because they use the original rollers to dye/print in the original manner. The imports are very stiff when purchased, with a characteristic scent of indigo dyes. Washing removes the stiffness and the fade pattern is likely to be the same as vintage fabrics. However, the thread count of the new imports is at a high of 74 threads per inch, and includes very even thread thickness and weave, where the antique versions are inconsistent in weave.

Other indigo reproductions made in the late twentieth century have a variety of characteristics that make differentiating them simple. Many indigo reproductions only approximate the depth of true indigo colors, but the patterns are very good repeats of nineteenth-century prints. For example, Harriet Hargrave's P&B Textiles collection, named Washday Blues, has 70 threads to the inch, and is an even weave with threads of even thickness. They do not ravel easily, and are moderately stiff to the hand. The surface was printed in a variety of blue shades reminiscent of indigo tones, but the reverse side is usually white, with a small bit of bleed-through of blue color – the reverse of antique indigo discharge prints.

Fons & Porter have provided Heritage and Heritage III. These are also of even weave, with very even thread thickness. The greige goods on the back reveal a predominantly tan cast. They are very stiff to the hand, even after repeated washings, which abraded the print on the surface.

Benartex's Documentaries and Sharon Newman's Timeless Treasures have a solid blue back, no bleed-through of surface pattern, with a white or cream face finish print on the front. The threads are of even thickness and weave. Documentaries has a 76 per inch thread count, and Timeless Treasures has 66.

When comparing overdyed greens made famous by Ely & Walker, the original antique prints show a wide variance of shade in green from piece to piece, even among fabrics of the same pattern. While the antique fabric examined appeared to have even twists in the warp threads, it was uneven in the weft, with 64 threads per inch. The fabric prints had clean, sharp edges when viewed through a linen tester. A comparison of ten different vintage double-dyed greens showed the back as a solid green or yellow-green, with the yellow pattern visible on the back and some black bleed-through.

The Callie Lu collection from South Sea Imports® by Kaye England appears very close to the original at first glance. Close examination shows the reproduction print had an indistinct edge, with feathering of dye color. Laurene Sinema's Legacies 1850s & Beyond, also from South Sea Imports, shows a white back with print bleed-through. Some reproductions feature a solid green without the yellow or black showing on the back. Both are distinctly different than the antiques.

Another color good for comparison was the popular chrome yellow from the 1850s onward. Besides the typical thread twist and weave examination, vintage prints of chrome yellow are yellow on the back with black and reds bleeding through, and are soft to the hand. Thread count varies widely, depending on the age of the antique. Reproductions of the chrome yellow-style prints at the end of the twentieth century show some with white backs and some with consistent yellow on the back, but without the black prints bleeding through at all.

In the Album Quilt line from Marcus Brothers Textiles by Judy Rothermel, there is a Turkey red-style print, featuring yellow, blue, and black ellipses on a red ground. The vintage piece has an uneven weave of 67 threads per inch. It has a crisp, clean print of yellow and blue that fills the entire space with a black that has red showing through at the edges of the threads, indicating that the red was applied first, and the black printed after. The reproduction sample has a slight misregistration, overlapping the yellow and blue portions onto the red, and leaving the omit exposed. This leaves a halo of white on the yellow, and the yellow appears more orange, while the blue overlaps onto the red, creating a purplish halo. The black portion of the print on the reproduction is very similar to that on the vintage piece. While the red color closely matches the vintage piece, the reproduction print is not as clear, and the yellow and blue portions are not as bright.

The Album Quilt reproduction fabric had a very even thread twist and weave of 76 threads per inch. The back of the fabric shows white on the reproduction, with some color bleed-through of all the print colors. The vintage example is pieced into a quilt so the back is not visible; however, a comparison with 12 other vintage pieces of this same Turkey red color with yellow, black, blue, and green prints shows a solid red back with bleed-through of black, yellow, blue, or green. A later edition of the same fabric reproduction by the same company shows a change in printing techniques and finishing, giving a softer hand and better registration, making the twist of thread and thread count the determining factors.

Many of the reproduction chintz styles have mostly plain backs with very little color bleed-through, while the originals may have strong colors coming through to the back, most especially in the golden yellows, teals, and blacks. Another factor to consider in comparing antiques from reproductions is the "hand," or texture, of the original. The evenness of fabric weave, the thread count, and the coloring medium and finish affect the hand of fabric. Quilters are tactile people. With some experience touching and comparing the old and the new, the texture of fabrics can give hints as to age.

Last but not least, the dyes and techniques used in 1800 and early 1900 quilts are not the same as the ones in common use today. They will age differently, and the colors will shift in varied ways we do not know yet. Some are already obvious, like fading in many of the blues, blacks, and reds of the early 1980s. (Craft prints only require 14 hours of colorfastness.)

*Black fabrics continue to experience shattering and shredding damage from dyes. Though it is usually sulfuric acid as opposed to tannic acid that does the damage at present, visible dye damage in black fabrics is not a reliable indicator of age.*

## IS IT AN AUTHENTIC ANTIQUE QUILT OR A REPRODUCTION?

There were a great number of period reproduction fabrics available from the 1980s continuing into the twenty-first century. This style is unlikely to abate for some time. Even if the fabric manufacturers were to cease tomorrow, most American quilters have a large collection, or deep stash, and could continue making quilts for years with what they have stored away.

For the inexperienced, telling a reproduction quilt from an authentic antique may be puzzling. While an assessment by a knowledgeable person can confirm or deny your suppositions, here are some comparisons between authentic and reproduction quilts to use on your own.

| AUTHENTIC VINTAGE | REPRODUCTION |
|---|---|
| Vintage quiltmakers often used what they had on hand. If the fabric had a misprint or a misregistration of the print, they still used it. | Quiltmakers of today usually do not use a fabric with an obvious flaw, but will cut around it, so as to avoid using it in their quilt. Most quilters will not purchase it. |
| Vintage quilts often have some small pieces sewn together of one color to make a large enough piece to fill a designated space. The print may not be the same, but the color usually was closely related. Borders are sometimes sewn in sections to make up the length. | Quiltmakers buy enough fabric to complete required areas with one fabric and no additional piecing. Most borders are cut of one long piece, with no seams. |

| AUTHENTIC VINTAGE | REPRODUCTION |
|---|---|

**AUTHENTIC VINTAGE**

Pieces were cut randomly, with little care taken for cutting along the grain of fabric in blocks. Warp and weft may travel in any direction, most obvious on plaids. Block-edge seams are just as likely to be on grain as not. Most sashing is straight of grain, but not always.

While decorative appliquéd or pieced borders were plentiful in vintage quilts, many times the turning of a corner was not thought out completely and planned before the work was done, and the design may turn awkwardly, or not at all. Top edges may appear incomplete.

Quilts before the mid-1840s had to be sewn by hand. After the 1850s, many blocks were hand-sewn, but were often set together by machine.

Machine topstitching appliqué and quilting were available from the 1870s onward. In the 1870–1890 period, machine quilting frequently consisted of straight lines across the quilt, or concentric echoes around appliqué designs. Sometimes the quilting was accomplished with a chain-stitch machine. Pre-quilted silk, straight-line or grid, was available from the 1870s onward, and was sometimes used to line coats and bonnets.

Early 1800s' quilts used minimal quilting on most printed fabric areas, which did not follow any piecing lines. Plain areas often featured very dense quilting. Quilts of the 1850s often have ornate quilting, with quilting over seam lines, and often include stuffed work, but almost all ornate quilting is performed on plain grounds. Quilting from the 1860–1890 period was often simple, with open spaces. Kit quilts of the twentieth century had preprinted quilting lines that related to the appliqué patterns.

**REPRODUCTION**

Modern techniques encourage the use of cutting on grain, or consistent use of straight grain along block edges. Plaids and stripes are often cut along grain lines, and are square to the block. The exceptions to straight-grain cuttings are for selective cutting to make optical illusions.

Often very conscious of today's design aesthetics, quiltmakers treat each quilt like a framed art piece, as if it were to hang upon the wall. Corners of borders are often very planned, whether pieced or appliquéd. Designs may be perfectly centered or on asymmetrical corners.

Sewing machines are the most common method of piecing quilts today. Blocks, sashing, borders, quilting, and one side of the binding are usually machine work.

Machine quilting is extremely varied, and often includes much curvilinear design. Overall repeat swirls or florals that follow no plan as to the piecing pattern are often quilted on an industrial machine, and usually found in quilts of the twentieth century or later. Quilts of the late 1980s and 1990s sometimes feature extensive closely packed quilting, known as stipple quilting in any number of patterns. Complex machine-quilted designs are frequent.

Much of the quilting from the 1960s through the 1980s includes patterns that outline the pieces at a ¼" distance. In the late 1980s and 1990s, quilting patterns were often chosen to enhance the effect of the piecing, including over seam lines.

| AUTHENTIC VINTAGE | REPRODUCTION |
|---|---|
| Pre-1850 quilts were most often pieced with natural, gray, or brown thread. Quilts from 1860 to 1870 frequently had brown thread. Black was most predominant for ca. 1900 quilts. Post-1900 quilts predominantly had ecru or off-white thread. Sometimes, a variety of thread colors was used within the same quilt, perhaps as a way to use up what was on hand. | Predominantly ecru or gray thread, or colors to match the fabrics being pieced for the piecing process, are used today. Quilt judges remark on contrasting threads for piecing because these are visible if markedly different. Quilters who regularly compete have learned to comply, and match thread to the fabrics being used. |
| Batting (filler) before 1960 was usually cotton, wool, or silk. Wool and cotton were clingy, and kept fabrics from sliding when the layers were rubbed against each other in a quilt. Silk was expensive, so it was rarely used. Many battings for better quilts before 1900 were thin, though some tied quilts and comforts were very thick. | Flannel sheeting and wool blankets were used for mid-twentieth century quilts. Many post-1963 quilts have polyester fiber that feels somewhat slimy in a quilt. The thickness of battings available varies. At the end of the 1990s, wool battings and poly-cotton battings gained favor. Black battings are sometimes used for dark quilts. |
| Early 1800s' quilts frequently have no binding, but were knife-edged and double-row stitched. Woven twill tape may have been used, especially in quilts from 1830 to 1850. Applied separate bindings of fabric are usually one layer, cut on straight grain. Corners use square joins, not mitered. Quilts with curved edges or corners are the exception, especially those from the 1920s to the 1930s, and may have used purchased bias binding instead of homemade. | In post-1980 quilts, the most common binding method is the double French binding, which uses two layers, may be bias cut, and often features a mitered, sewn corner. Joins of strips are also usually mitered and pressed open to reduce bulk, making joins more challenging to find. Bindings are usually machine sewn on one side and hand finished on the other. Completely machine-sewn bindings are frequent. |
| If it's red, it's red. If it's pink...it's red. Black grounds and chocolate grounds are interchangeable. Any green is green, and purple is purple no matter what shade of purple it is. | Today's quilters want everything to match, or be as random as possible. "Make-do" color placement is very unusual. |

# Glossary

**Art quilt** – A quilt designed and produced specifically for the design elements as they relate to artistic expression. Any technique or materials might apply. Workmanship may be poor to fine as compared to traditional standards.

**Bark cloth** – A rough-surfaced fabric of cotton or linen, or other rough fiber, that is stiff to the hand before washing. It was used mainly for upholstery or curtains during the 1940s through the early 1960s. It frequently was recycled into tied comforts during the 1950s to the 1960s.

**Batik** – Fabric ornamented by the hand application of resists and dying. Usually imported to the United States from Bali or other Far Eastern countries.

**Block of the month** – A group of blocks, often made by varied individuals, following a prescribed pattern. These are often made as part of quilt guild activities or as purchasable kits from quilt stores.

**Challenge quilt** – A quilt or group of quilts having a theme or fabric in common, which each participant is required to make, following a given set of rules.

**Colorway** – The use of one set of rollers or screens to produce the same pattern in a variety of colors in order to please most purchasers for the least amount of expenditure.

**Contemporary quilt** – A contemporary quilt is a quilt made at the present time. Increasing numbers of contemporary quilts are being made in the art-quilt style. Many traditional-style quilts are greatly influenced by art quilts, and the distinction between the two decreases after 1990.

**Crocking** – Damage to dyed patterns caused by friction to the fabric surface.

**Dope dyed** – Dyed in the solution before passing through the spinneret; used for synthetic fibers.

**Dupioni** – A woven fiber that utilizes filament silk for warp with a filler weft of raw slubbed silk from conjoined silk cocoons.

**Embellishment** – A term applied in the 1980s and after to describe ornamentation added to quilts and wearable art. This might include threadwork, buttons, ribbons, beading, fringing, dimensional appliqué, ruffling, or tucking.

**Fugitive dye** – Unstable dye that tends to run, fade, or change colors. Sometimes a fugitive dye will bleed onto nearby fabrics.

**Grinning** – White spaces created by poor registration in the printing process.

**Haloing** – A planned white space around print motifs allowing faster printing due to the lack of need for precise placement of motifs.

**Kit quilts** – Quilt patterns that are designed and sold for profit, including fabric, directions, embroidery thread, and other possible required elements. These were sold through newspaper advertisements and catalogs, such as Herschners and Paragon. Many manufactured kits include blue dot markings that cannot be removed. More recently, kits are sold through quilt shops or mail order, but may not have blue-line pattern printing. Kits include block-of-the-month quilts.

**Lamé** – A woven fiber that is metallic in appearance. It may have cotton, silk, or polyester as the warp because the metallic weft fibers are usually low in tensile strength.

**Reproduction** – The copying of a fabric pattern formerly in use in the appropriate color combination to use as a duplicate or replacement for the original. Sometimes made in several colorways, with only the document colorway close to the original as an accurate reproduction. See *colorway.*

**Rotary cutter** – An instrument first designed for paper cutting, imported to the United States in 1979. The blade is made of tungsten steel and is razor sharp. By rolling the cutter along a hard guiding edge, quiltmakers cut several layers of fabrics at one time. With a companion self-healing cutting mat and clear acrylic rulers, it revolutionized piecing techniques in the 1980s and beyond.

**Round robin** – A quilt made by a group of persons, each taking their turn at adding a new element to the piece to complete it.

**Screen printing** – A method of transferring pattern to greige goods. Performed by hand in small specialty shops, the process is also the base for producing large print runs in the manufacturing industry.

**Spinneret** – An item used during the production of manmade fibers, specifically, with fine holes that the polymer solution passes to form a thin fiber. It may be cold or hot drawn. Based on the principle of spiders and caterpillars that form their fiber through a spinneret.

**Step gradation** – A group of fabrics, usually colored with fiber-reactive dyes, which are a progressive step darker in each piece. The range is most often six or eight steps, and may have been sold as a bundle of folded fabrics displaying all the shades. Frequently dyed in the home setting, or by small home-based entrepreneurs.

**Thread play** – Embellishment methods utilizing sewing machines and a wide variety of colors and/or types of thread as the decorative element. The title of embellishment style taught by Libby Lehman, Sharee Dawn Roberts, and others. Freehand machine embroidery.

**Traditional quilt** – A quilt pieced or appliquéd using patterns and techniques, the style generally reminiscent of pre-1930 quilts.

**Wearable art** – Clothing made to wear, but featuring any of the effects used in making quilts as art, including fabric manipulation, ribbons, machine embroidery, beading, or button embellishment, and sometimes featuring nonstandard base-pattern cuts.

*Dating Fabrics 2: A Color Guide 1950–2000*

# Bibliography

*American Quilter Magazine* (various). Paducah, KY: American Quilter's Society, 1984–2000.

Atkins, Jacqueline. *America's Quilts.* Lincolnwood, IL: Publications International, 1990.

Bacon, Lenice Ingram. *American Patchwork Quilts.* New York: William Morrow and Company, 1973.

Bishop, Robert, Karey P. Bresenhan, and Bonnie Leman. *Hands All Around, Quilts From Many Nations.* New York: E.P. Dutton, 1987.

Bishop, Robert and Carter Houck. *All Flags Flying.* New York: E.P. Dutton, 1986.

Bosker, Gideon, John Gramstad, and Michele Mancini. *Fabulous Fabrics of the Fifties (and Other Terrific Textiles of the '20s, '30s and '40s).* San Francisco: Chronicle Books, 1992.

Brackman, Barbara. *Patterns of Progress: Quilts in the Machine Age.* Los Angeles: Autry Museum of Western Heritage, 1997.

Bullard, Lacy Folmar. *Quilts from Colonial to Contemporary.* Lincolnwood, IL: Publications International, 1992.

Campbell, Patricia and Mimi Ayers. *Jacobean Appliqué, Book II.* Paducah, KY: American Quilter's Society, 1995.

Campbell-Harding, Valerie and Michele Walker. *Every Kind of Patchwork. Tunbridge Wells,* Kent: Search Press, 1978.

Colby, Averil. *Patchwork.* Boston: Charles T. Branford Co., 1958.

_____. *Patchwork Quilts.* New York: Charles Scribner and Sons, 1965.

_____. *Quilting.* New York: Charles Scribner and Sons, 1971.

Collins, Sally. *Small Scale Quiltmaking.* Lafayette, CA: C&T Publishing, 1996.

Denton, Susan, and Barbara Macey. *Quiltmaking.* New York: Sterling Publishing, 1988.

Ettinger, Roseann. *50s Popular Fashions for Men, Women, Boys and Girls.* Atglen, PA: Schiffer Publishing, 1995.

_____. *Fifties Forever.* Atglen, PA: Schiffer Publishing, 1998.

Faoro, Victoria, ed. *Award Winning Quilts and Their Makers, volumes I–IV.* Paducah, KY: American Quilter's Society, 1991–1994.

Fisher, Richard and Dorothy Wolfthal. *Textile Print Design.* New York: Fairchild Publications, 1987.

Fons, Marianne and Liz Porter. *Quilters Complete Guide.* Birmingham, AL: Oxmoor House, 1993.

Green, Sylvia. *Patchwork for Beginners.* New York: Watson-Guptill Publications, 1972.

Gutcheon, Beth. *The Perfect Patchwork Primer.* Baltimore, MD: Penguin Books, 1974.

Gutcheon, Beth and Jeffrey Gutcheon. *The Quilt Design Workbook.* New York: Rawson Associates, Publishers, Inc., 1976.

Hinson, Delores A. *Quilting Manual.* New York: Hearthside Press, Inc., 1966.

Hollen, Norma and Jane Saddler. *Textiles, Fourth Edition.* New York: MacMillan and Colliers, 1973.

Holstein, Jonathan. *American Pieced Quilts.* New York: Viking, 1972.

Ickis, Margerite. *The Standard Book of Quilt Making and Collecting.* New York: Dover Publications, 1949.

# Bibliography

Jarnow, Jill. *The Patchwork Point of View.* New York: Simon & Schuster, 1975.

Kadolph, Sara J. and Anna L. Langford. *Textiles, Ninth Edition.* Upper Saddle River, NJ: Prentice Hall, 2002.

Korosec, Constance, and Leslie Pina. *Naturally '70s Fabrics.* Atglen, PA: Schiffer Publishing, 2000.

_____. *The Synthetic '70s Fabric of the Decade.* Atglen, PA: Schiffer Publishing, 1999.

*Lady's Circle Patchwork Quilts* (various). New York, NY: Lopez Publishing, 1973–1997.

Laury, Jean Ray. *Quilts and Coverlets, A Contemporary Approach.* New York: Van Nostrand Reinhold, 1970.

Lyle, Dorothy S. *Modern Textiles, Second Edition.* John Wiley & Sons, 1982.

Mahler, Celine Blanchard. *Once Upon a Quilt.* New York: Van Nostrand Reinhold, 1973.

Masopust, Katie Pasquini. *Fractured Landscape Quilts.* Lafayette, CA: C&T Publishing, 1996.

McMorris, Penny and Michael Kile. *The Art Quilt.* San Francisco: Quilt Digest Press, 1986.

Museum of American Folk Art. *Discover America and Friends Sharing America.* New York: Dutton Books, 1991.

Newman, Thelma. *Quilting, Patchwork, Appliqué and Trapunto: Traditional Methods and Original Designs.* New York: Crown Publishers, 1974.

O'Donnol, Shirley Miles. *American Costume 1915–1970.* Bloomington, IN: Indiana University Press, 1982.

*Patchwork Patter* (various). Ellicott City, MD: National Quilting Association, 1983–1995.

*Quilt World* (various). Seabrook, NH: House of White Birches, 1976–1996.

*Quilter's Newsletter Magazine* (various). Bonnie Leman, ed., Wheatridge, CO: Quilter's Newsletter, 1969–2000.

Ramsey, Bets, and Gail Andrews Trechsel. *Southern Quilts: A New View.* McLean, VA: EPM Publications, 1991.

Rogers, Janet, ed. *Visions: Quilt Art.* Lafayette, CA: C&T Publishing, 1997.

Safford, Carleton and Robert Bishop. *America's Quilts and Coverlets.* New York, NY: E.P. Dutton and Co., Inc., 1972.

Schoeser, Mary. *Fabrics and Wallpapers, Twentieth Century Design.* London: Bell and Hyman Limited, 1986.

Shih, Joy. *Funky Fabrics of the '60s.* Atglen, PA: Schiffer Publishing, 1996.

Skinner, Tina. *Abstract Textile Designs.* Atglen, PA: Schiffer Publishing, 1998.

_____. *Designer Fabrics of the Early '60s.* Atglen, PA: Schiffer Publishing, 1998.

_____. *Dots: A Pictorial Essay on Pointed, Printed Fabrics.* Atglen, PA: Schiffer Publishing, 1998.

_____. *Fashionable Clothing from the Sears Catalogs: Mid 1950s.* Atglen, PA: Schiffer Publishing, 2002.

_____. *Flower Power Prints from the 1960s.* Atglen, PA: Schiffer Publishing, 1998.

Timby, Deborah Bird, ed. and Quilt San Diego. *Visions: Quilts of a New Decade.* San Diego, CA: C&T Publishing, 1990.

Timmons, Christine, ed. *The New Quilt I: Dairy Barn Quilt National.* Newton, CT: Taunton Press, 1991.

Wingate, Isabel B. *Textile Fabrics and Their Selection, Seventh Edition.* Englewood Cliffs, NJ: Prentice Hall, 1976.

Wooster, Ann-Sargent. *Quiltmaking, The Modern Approach to a Traditional Craft.* New York: Drake Publishers, 1972.

# Eileen Jahnke Trestain

Eileen Jahnke Trestain is a lifelong textile enthusiast, having been raised in a family of seamstresses. Her parents ran a home-based business of sewing machines, fabrics, and classes. Eileen and her husband, David, have carried on the tradition. Together, they have produced patterns for the former company, Peonies Needlework, and at present for Dream House Quilts. They have produced block-of-the-month study quilts, based on a series of concepts provided by Judy Roche and Corinne Kramer. Eileen researches and writes, and Dave is the computer wizard who creates the graphics.

Eileen is a certified appraiser of quilted textiles. Her work has been published in varied venues, including *British Patchwork & Quilting*, *Miniworks Magazine*, and Rodale's *Favorite Techniques from the Experts*. She has been featured on the television show *Simply Quilts* and on Nebraska public television. In 2000, Classic Cottons produced two lines of reproduction fabrics, with Eileen as the curatorial advisor.

For two years, Eileen served as the collection manager for the Clark County Historical Museum in Vancouver, Washington. She designed and installed exhibits for the museum, and led a staff of volunteers in caring for treasures of Pacific Northwest history. Her present hobby is historical reenactment, portraying 1845 pioneer Esther Short, on whose land claim downtown Vancouver, Washington, now resides. Daughters Patricia and Carolina also participate as part of the Vancouver Heritage ambassadors, and they volunteer at historic Fort Vancouver National Park.

# Other AQS Books

This is only a small selection of the books available from the American Quilter's Society. AQS books are known worldwide for timely topics, clear writing, beautiful color photos, and accurate illustrations and patterns. The following books are available from your local bookseller, quilt shop, or public library.

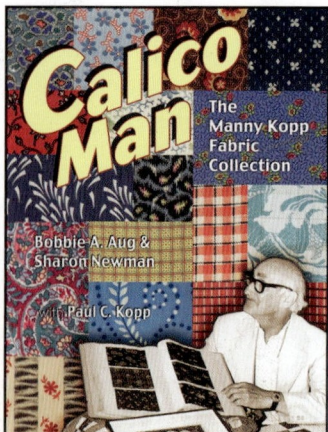

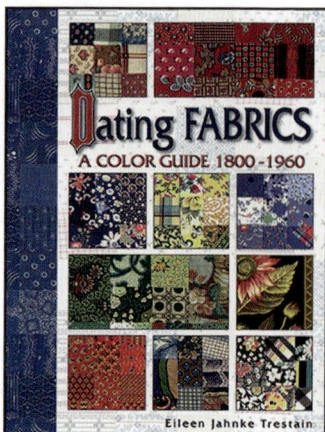

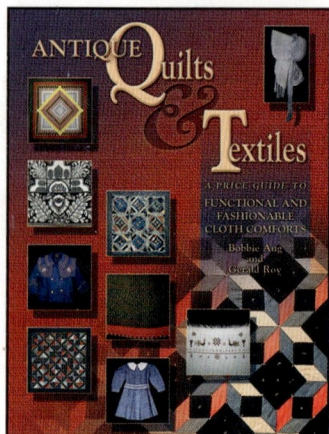

LOOK for these books nationally.

Call **1-800-626-420** or VISIT our Web site at

## www.AmericanQuilter.com